CAPITALIZE ON
Retirement

Make the Most of Your Life Savings With
Capital A Wealth Management

David Domenick Jr.
and Brandon Domenick

Copyright © 2022 by Capital A Wealth Management.

All rights reserved. No part of this publication may be reproduced, distributed, or transmitted in any form or by any means, including photocopying, recording, or other electronic or mechanical methods, without the prior written permission of the publisher, except in the case of brief quotations embodied in critical reviews and certain other noncommercial uses permitted by copyright law. For permission requests, write to the publisher at the address below. These materials are provided to you by Capital A Wealth Management for informational purposes only and Capital A Wealth Management and Advisors Excel, LLC expressly disclaim any and all liability arising out of or relating to your use of same. The provision of these materials does not constitute legal or investment advice and does not establish an attorney-client relationship between you and Capital A Wealth Management. No tax advice is contained in these materials. You are solely responsible for ensuring the accuracy and completeness of all materials as well as the compliance, validity, and enforceability of all materials under any applicable law. The advice and strategies found within may not be suitable for every situation. You are expressly advised to consult with a qualified attorney or other professional in making any such determination and to determine your legal or financial needs. No warranty of any kind, implied, expressed, or statutory, including but not limited to the warranties of title and non-infringement of third-party rights, is given with respect to this publication.

Capital A Wealth Management
8050 Rowan Road, Suite 602, Cranberry Twp, PA 16066
312 N Jefferson Street, New Castle, PA 16101
www.CapitalAInvestments.com

Book layout ©2021 Advisors Excel, LLC

Capitalize on Retirement/Capital A Wealth Management — 1st edition

ISBN 9798840012284

David Domenick Jr. and Brandon Domenick are registered as Investment Advisor Representatives and are licensed insurance agents in the state of Pennsylvania. Capital A Wealth Management is an independent financial services firm that helps individuals create retirement strategies using a variety of investment and insurance products to custom suit their needs and objectives.

Capital A Wealth Management is an independent financial services firm that utilizes a variety of investment and insurance products. Securities offered only by duly registered individuals through Madison Avenue Securities, LLC (MAS), member FINRA/SIPC. Investment advisory services offered only by duly registered individuals through AE Wealth Management, LLC (AEWM), a Registered Investment Adviser. MAS and David A. Domenick or Capital A Wealth Management are not affiliated entities. AEWM and David A. Domenick or Capital A Wealth Management are not affiliated entities.

The contents of this book are provided for informational purposes only and are not intended to serve as the basis for any financial decisions. Any tax, legal, or estate planning information is general in nature. It should not be construed as legal or tax advice. Always consult an attorney or tax professional regarding the applicability of this information to your unique situation.

Information presented is believed to be factual and up-to-date, but we do not guarantee its accuracy, and it should not be regarded as a complete analysis of the subjects discussed. All expressions of opinion are those of the author as of the date of publication and are subject to change. Content should not be construed as personalized investment advice nor should it be interpreted as an offer to buy or sell any securities mentioned. A financial advisor should be consulted before implementing any of the strategies presented.

Investing involves risk, including the potential loss of principal. No investment strategy can guarantee a profit or protect against loss in periods of declining values. Any references to protection benefits or guaranteed/lifetime income streams refer only to fixed insurance products, not securities or investment products. Insurance and annuity product guarantees are backed by the financial strength and claims-paying ability of the issuing insurance company.

Any names used in the examples in this book are hypothetical only and do not represent actual clients.

"Often, when you think you're at the end of something, you're at the beginning of something else."

~ Fred Rogers

To our father, David Sr., who inspired us to take this path and instilled in us, above all else, the importance of helping others, to the best of our abilities, succeed in achieving their goals and dreams.

Table of Contents

The Importance of Planning i
Longevity 1
Taxes 21
Market Volatility 29
Retirement Income 37
Social Security 53
401(k)s & IRAs 67
Annuities 77
Estate & Legacy 85
Women Retire Too 93
Long-Term Care Insurance 107
Finding a Financial Professional 113
Acknowledgments 117
About the Author 119

PREFACE
The Importance of Planning

At some point, you've probably seen an advertisement for a retirement planner who talks about helping you reach "your number," implying that once you've accumulated this specific amount, you'll be set for life and in a good position to stop working forever.

As financial advisors, the people who walk through our door for the first time frequently follow this line of thinking. While we agree *saving* more can translate to *doing* more in retirement, comprehensive financial planning isn't always that cut and dried.

One recent example was a nurse, who had a number in mind that's very common among pre-retirees: $1 million. She was just a few thousand dollars away from achieving this milestone in her 401(k) and, therefore, planned to keep working until she reached it.

Unfortunately, the COVID-19 pandemic put her, and so many others, in an unexpected position. No field was impacted by this crisis more than medical professionals, and this nurse obviously had plenty of things to worry about at that time. She hoped money wouldn't be one of them.

However, before coming to meet with us, she was managing all financial decisions on her own. During the market crash in March 2020, she panicked and sold many of her assets. When the dust settled, she lost 40 percent of her accumulated wealth.

Someone who was so close to retiring — and frankly deserved to based on the work she put in during the pandemic — now had no choice but to continue working and recouping her losses.

The lesson of this story is that it doesn't matter what the number is in your accounts if you don't take the time to create a proper financial strategy. In our opinion, accumulating is the easy part. Knowing how to use your savings is more difficult. That's where we come in.

At Capital A Wealth Management, we focus on giving the people we work with a course they can stay on to and through retirement. We call this process our Alpha Plan.

Alpha Plan

With the Alpha Plan, we focus on five key areas of retirement planning, while taking the time to learn about your individual situation and needs, before proceeding to create a customized strategy that helps you achieve your financial goals.

The attention we pay to these five areas is designed to help ensure your finances are optimized in all facets of retirement:

- Income planning
  We evaluate your current financial situation and seek to optimize Social Security and pension payouts to help ensure your monthly expenses can be paid reliably now and decades down the road.
- Investment planning
  Based on your risk tolerance and risk capacity, we can offer a wide range of funds and equities to create a cost-efficient portfolio that fits your objectives.
- Tax planning strategies
  We aim to minimize the taxes owed by you, and your next of kin after you pass away, whether it's income taxes, capital gain taxes, or estate taxes.
- Legacy planning
  Through our strategic partnerships with trusted estate planning attorneys, we can help you clearly establish beneficiaries and avoid probate to help ensure your loved ones receive the highest amount possible.

- Healthcare planning
  Whether you're looking for the right Medicare option or concerned about the high costs of long-term care, we take the time to walk you through a system that can be overwhelming.

The Alpha Plan, and the name of our business itself, are both nods to our father, David A. Domenick, who first opened this business as David A. Domenick Investments back in 1990. We're proud to say our door has been open to residents and neighbors of the Northern Pittsburgh area ever since.

Those who grew up with our dad and those who work closely with him call him by his nickname and middle initial: "A." As his sons, when we joined the business, we wanted to honor that shorthand nickname, which is why we're now known as Capital A Wealth Management.

Unlike a lot of financial advisors who start with product talk and work backward from there, we take the time to understand your needs before building a plan. In our first meeting with new clients, we go through all of the goals someone has for their time and money in retirement.

In our second meeting, we start to talk about possible strategies, and finally, the last step is to explain the financial vehicles that we believe can help put them in the best position to achieve the lifestyle they're hoping for. For some of our clients, this could mean an annuity with its guaranteed income stream. For you, it could be something completely different.

We like to say we put the goals before the tolls. Once your goals are established, the tolls fall into place.

One of our favorite examples of this was with a man who we'll call Bruce. During our initial strategy session with him, we were asking questions, and getting to know him while he got to know us, and we asked him what his goals were. He had one right off the bat: he wanted a new Corvette.

So, we knew from the beginning this was one of his key retirement goals. As far as finances were concerned, he was an average pre-retiree. He didn't have $5 million or $10 million to his name, but he was happy with his current lifestyle and didn't mind working a couple more years to continue saving.

When we meet with clients, we look at every available piece of information and assess each of their accounts to get a full picture of their financial situation. Most importantly, we explain everything to the clients so they recognize where they stand. In Bruce's case, his finances were in much better shape than he expected, and we had the pleasure of telling him he'd be able to afford that dream car.

This was a new Corvette that was on back-order for nearly a year. The car just arrived recently, and Bruce drove it down to our office for us to see it and took us for a ride. It was just an awesome experience to see that.

Achieving your goals is a rewarding side of retirement planning, but of course, it's also important to prepare for the unexpected costs that aren't as fun. With older age comes more health expenses, and the earlier you anticipate those costs, the better. Some people question why they should bother preparing for a potential downturn in financial health or physical health when there's no way of knowing when (or if) that will ever occur. Hopefully, it never will!

However, we usually compare financial planning to buying auto insurance or homeowners insurance. Choosing the investment that's most appropriate for your situation is like insuring your retirement. Yes, there is a cost up front, but if something unforeseen happens, you'll be glad you had a plan in place.

This planning is especially important as lifespans continue to grow. It's common today for people to live well into their eighties, and for that reason, we feel it's better to hope for the best and plan for the worst.

Sometimes people come in and say, "I'll probably only live to age seventy because my mother and father both passed away young." We warn people not to plan for that. In some ways, if you plan to live to seventy, and are still around at ninety, that's a good thing. However, that scenario could lead to some financial issues. Planning to live to ninety helps ensure you don't run out of money with twenty years left in retirement.

When planning is done right, the result can be quite the contrast from the story about the nurse we opened this chapter with. We're fortunate enough to see our clients retire regularly, and the months leading up to March 2020 were no exception.

The economic crash of that surreal month was a shock to everyone, but imagine the concern if you had just retired as the COVID-19 outbreak began. For some, that's exactly what happened. There are a lot of risks outside of your control that could be detrimental to your savings, even in years when there isn't a pandemic. However, we believe those who plan and stay the course can maintain financial confidence, knowing their planning takes any outcome, even an unforeseen global pandemic, into account.

Potential Risks to Your Ideal Retirement

Ever feel like life gets in the way and prevents you from doing things you should not ignore? If we're honest with ourselves, we've all put off obligations we know are important.

In your case, you may be reading this book because it's time to get serious about financial planning and, specifically, devising a way to best prepare for retirement. A retirement income plan should be based on more components than just your investments or your finances. The preparation of that strategy begins with your desires, ambitions, and goals for this fulfilling season of life.

There's no such thing as a silly question. Not when one of the most common questions we hear from folks regarding retirement is, "Am I going to be okay?" Often, it seems, people are reluctant to meet with financial professionals because they worry they might sound uneducated. Yet, it's understandable for you to be a novice when it comes to financial issues and retirement concerns. You've been busy with your lives and your careers. Time spent away from work has meant time spent being around those you love and engaging in the activities you enjoy. Retirement provides the opportunity to do even more of that, while not fretting over work obligations.

Concerns people have about what they may encounter during retirement can be far-reaching and still perfectly legitimate. For a quick snapshot, we want to provide a brief sampling of wide-ranging issues that can come up during discussions about what to potentially brace for in retirement. This book will touch on many of these issues in further detail.

Politics: A presidential election often stirs emotions regarding potential effects on the economy. Investors grow anxious about how a new president can influence market returns. It's Congress, however, that establishes tax laws and passes spending bills. Yet the president can indirectly affect the economy and the stock market in various ways such as the appointment of policymakers, development of international relations, and influential sway on new legislation.

Taxes: An example of a president's influence can be cited in signature legislation passed during Donald Trump's presidency, the Tax Cuts and Jobs Act of 2017. However, our tax system remains progressive, so the more you earn, the higher the tax rate within each tax bracket of subsequently higher income. A thorough understanding of tax regulations can be crucial. A financial professional can help identify potential issues a tax professional can help solve.

Divorce: A fair and equitable division of retirement assets can be difficult to settle, especially if one spouse has contributed most of the funds while the other spouse stayed at home to care for family. A financial professional, often in concert with a divorce attorney, not only can help you navigate the distribution of retirement assets but also identify whether a divorce might leave you with a shortfall of retirement savings.

Inflation: Government spending, which most recently spiked with relief packages designed to assist U.S. citizens during the COVID-19 pandemic, can fuel concerns of inflationary hikes stemming from an influx of money thrust at the same consumer goods. A retiree's income can be jeopardized by the effect inflation can have on a fixed budget.

The value of currency decreases because inflation erodes purchasing power.

Health pandemic: The coronavirus outbreak could impact how Americans view risks and re-examine healthy habits. That, potentially, could be one of the effects of COVID-19 as we assess how long a pandemic can last and if others will occur in our lifetimes. The cost of health care can be surprising throughout retirement. It could become an issue people focus on even more following the pandemic, which had a particularly acute impact on some U.S. elder care facilities.

Cybersecurity: Think you'll give up your smartphone in retirement? No way, right? It's here to stay, along with other intellectual gadgetry, including devices that have not been patented or invented. Retirees are becoming more tech-savvy, yet they can also be more trusting, which can be problematic when responding to potential scammers by phone, text, or email. Cybercrime often uses technology to target potential victims. Scammers, much like technology, figure to only grow more sophisticated over time.

CHAPTER 1

Longevity

You would think the prospect of the grave would loom more frightening as we age, yet many retirees say their number one concern is actually running out of money in their twilight years.[1] This fear is, unfortunately, justified, in part, because of one significant factor: We're living longer.

According to the Social Security Administration, in 1950, the average life expectancy for a sixty-five-year-old man was seventy-eight, and the average for a sixty-five-year-old woman was eighty-one. In 2021, those averages were eighty-three and eighty-eight, respectively.[2]

The bottom line of many retirees' budget woes comes down to this: They just didn't plan to live so long. Now, when we are younger and in our working years, that's not something we necessarily see as a bad thing; don't some people fantasize about living forever or, at least, reaching the ripe old age of one hundred?

However, with a longer lifespan, as we near retirement, we face a few snags. Our resources are finite—we only have so much money to provide income—but our lifespans can be

---

[1] Liz Weston. nerdwallet.com. March 25, 2021. "Will You Really Run Out of Money in Retirement?"
https://www.nerdwallet.com/article/finance/will-you-really-run-out-of-money-in-retirement

[2] Social Security Administration. 2011 Trustees Report. "Actuarial Publications: Cohort Life Expectancy."
https://www.ssa.gov/OACT/TR/2011/lr5a4.html

unpredictably long, perhaps longer than our resources allow. Also, longer lives don't necessarily equate with healthier lives. The longer you live, the more money you will likely need to spend on health care, even excluding long-term care needs like nursing homes.

You will also run into inflation. If you don't plan to live another twenty-five years but end up doing so, inflation at an average 3 percent will approximately double the price of goods over that time period. Put a harsh twist on that and the buying power of a ninety-year-old will be half of what they possessed if they retired at sixty-five.[3] And this is before you count the expenses of any potential health care or long-term care needs.

Because we don't necessarily get to have our cake and eat it, too, our collective increased longevity hasn't necessarily increased the healthy years of our lives. Typically, our life-extending care most widely applies to the time in our lives where we will need more care in general. Think of common situations like a pacemaker at eighty-five, or cancer treatment at seventy-eight.

"Wow, guys," we can hear you say. "Way to start with the good news first."

We know, we've painted a grim picture, but all we're concerned about here is cost. It's hard to put a dollar sign on life, but that is essentially what we're talking about when discussing longevity and finances. According to the Stanford Center on Longevity, more than half of pre-retirees underestimate the life expectancy of the average sixty-five-year-old.[4] Living longer isn't a bad thing; it just costs more, and one key to a sound retirement strategy is preparing for it in advance.

---

[3] Bob Sullivan, Benjamin Curry. Forbes. April 28, 2021. "Inflation And Retirement Investments: What You Need to Know." https://www.forbes.com/advisor/retirement/inflation-retirement-investments

[4] Stanford Center on Longevity. "Underestimating Years in Retirement." http://longevity.stanford.edu/underestimating-years-in-retirement

One couple we serve, who we'll call Jim and Sarah, always wanted to retire at age sixty-five, and therefore they did everything they could do to save and put every little penny extra into their retirement accounts. The reason they wanted to retire at sixty-five is because they really loved to travel. When they traveled, this is when they felt the most free and fulfilled.

Part of our planning for clients who have a passion for traveling is to map out how much they plan to spend on travel throughout the year. We can account for the small weekend trips they want to take, while also allocating for those special trips with the entire family that may happen just once or twice a year.

When frequent travelers plan ahead for trips and budget them in advance, they may have an easier time enjoying the journey without worry about overspending. Sometimes, the best thing you can do is put a plan in place and let your hard-earned dollars work for you.

Retiring Early

A key part of planning for retirement revolves around retirement income. After all, retirement is cutting the cord that tethers you to your employer—and your monthly check. However, that check often comes with many other benefits, particularly health care. Health care is often the thing that can unexpectedly put dreams for an early retirement on hold. Some employers offer health benefits to their retired workers, but that number has declined drastically over the past several decades. In 1988, among employers who offered health benefits to their workers, 66 percent offered health benefits to their retirees. In 2020, that number was 29 percent.[5]

---

[5] Henry J. Kaiser Family Foundation. October 8, 2020. "2020 Employer Health Benefits Survey Section Eleven: Retiree Health Benefits." https://www.kff.org/report-section/ehbs-2020-section-11-retiree-health-benefits

So, with employer-offered retirement health benefits on the wane, this becomes a major point of concern for anyone who is looking to retire, particularly those who are looking to retire before age sixty-five, when they would become eligible for Medicare coverage. In 2021, Fidelity estimated that the average retired couple at age sixty-five will need approximately $300,000 for medical expenses, not including long-term care.[6] Do you think it's likely that cost will decrease?

Even if you are working until age sixty-five or have plans to cover your health expenses until that point, we often have clients who incorrectly assume Medicare is their golden ticket to cover all expenses. That is simply not the case.

Retiring Later

Planning for a long life in retirement partly depends on when you retire. While many people end up retiring earlier than they anticipated—due to injuries, layoffs, family crises, and other unforeseen circumstances—continuing to work past age sixty (and even sixty-five) is still a viable option for others and can be an excellent way to help establish financial comfort in retirement.

There are many reasons for this. For one, you obviously still earn a paycheck and the benefits accompanying it. Medical coverage and beefing up your retirement accounts with further savings can be significant by themselves but continuing your income also should keep you from dipping into your retirement funds, further allowing them the opportunity to grow.

Additionally, for many workers, their nine-to-five job is more than just clocking in and out. Having a sense of purpose can keep us active physically, mentally, and socially. That kind of activity and level of engagement may also help stave off many of the health problems that plague retirees. Avoiding a

---

[6] Fidelity Viewpoints. Fidelity. May 6, 2021. "How to Plan for Rising Health Care Costs." https://www.fidelity.com/viewpoints/personal-finance/plan-for-rising-health-care-costs

sedentary life is one of the advantages of staying plugged into the workforce, if possible.

Let's talk about Dave Sr., the founder of Capital A Wealth Management and our father. Our father has helped hundreds of retirees prepare for successful retirements throughout his career. He has always enjoyed working with people and gets a lot of satisfaction out of helping individuals and families navigate the pitfalls of retirement. Although Dave Sr. has been fortunate and can retire whenever he would like, he still loves helping our great communities retire successfully.

He has always had a knack for helping others and this work is what fulfills him in life. We often tell Dad to take some time off and go enjoy his life, but he's most fulfilled when he's helping other people and giving back his wealth of knowledge to the advisors in our organization and our great client base.

Health Care

Take a second to reflect on your health care plan. Although working up to or even past age sixty-five would allow you to avoid a coverage gap between your working years and Medicare, that may not be an option for you. Even if it is, when you retire, you will need to make some decisions about what kind of insurance coverage you may need to supplement your Medicare. Are there any medical needs you have that may require coverage in addition to Medicare? Did your parents or grandparents have any inherited medical conditions you might consider using a special savings plan to cover?

These are all questions that are important to review with your financial professional so you can be sure you have enough money put aside for health care.

Long-Term Care

Longevity means the need for long-term care is statistically more likely to happen. If you intend to pass on a legacy, planning for long-term care is paramount, since most estimates project nearly 70 percent of Americans will need some type of it.[7] However, this may be one of the biggest, most stressful pieces of longevity planning we encounter in our work. For one thing, who wants to talk about the point in their lives when they may feel the most limited? Who wants to dwell on what will happen if they no longer can toilet, bathe, dress, or feed themselves?

We get it; this is a less-than-fun part of planning. But a little bit of preparation now can go a long way!

When it comes to your longevity, just like with your goals, one of the important things to do is sit and dream. It may not be the fun, road-trip-to-the-Grand-Canyon kind of dreaming, but you can spend time envisioning how you want your twilight years to look.

For instance, if it is important for you to live in your home for as long as possible, who will provide for the day-to-day fixes and to-dos of housework if you become ill? Will you set aside money for a service, or do you have relatives or friends nearby whom you could comfortably allow to help you? Do you prefer in-home care over a nursing home or assisted living? This could be a good time to discuss the possibility of moving into a retirement community versus staying where you are or whether it's worth moving to another state and leaving relatives behind.

These are all important factors to discuss with your spouse and children, as *now* is the right time to address questions and concerns. For instance, is aging in place more important to one spouse than the other? Are the friends or relatives who live nearby emotionally, physically, and financially capable of helping you for a time if you face an illness?

Many families we meet with find these conversations very uncomfortable, particularly when children discuss nursing home care with their parents. A knee-jerk reaction for many is to promise they will care for their aging parents. This is noble

---

[7] LongTermCare.gov. February 18, 2020. "How Much Care Will You Need?" https://acl.gov/ltc/basic-needs/how-much-care-will-you-need

and well-intentioned, but there needs to be an element of realism here. Does "help" from an adult child mean they stop by and help you with laundry, cooking, home maintenance, and bills? Or does it mean they move you into their spare room when you have hip surgery? Are they prepared to help you use the restroom and bathe if that becomes difficult for you to do on your own?

We don't mean to discourage families from caring for their own; this can be a profoundly admirable relationship when it works out. However, we've seen families put off planning for late-in-life care based on a tenuous promise that the adult children would care for their parents, only to watch as the support system crumbles. Sometimes this is because the assumed caregiver hasn't given serious thought to the preparation they would need, both in a formal sense and regarding their personal physical, emotional, and financial commitments. This is often also because we can't see the future: Alzheimer's disease and other maladies of old age can exact a heavy toll. When a loved one reaches the point where he or she is at risk of wandering away or needs help with two or more activities of daily living, it can be more than one person or family can realistically handle.

If you know what you want, communicate with your family about both the best-case and worst-case scenarios. Then, hope for the best, and plan for the worst.

Realistic Cost of Care

Wrapped up in your planning should be a consideration for the cost of long-term care. One study estimates that by 2030, the nation's long-term care costs could reach $2.5 trillion as roughly 24 million Americans require some type of long-term care.[8] The potential costs for such care and treatment can be

---

[8] Tara O'Neill Hayes, Sara Kurtovic. Americanactionforum.org. February 18, 2020. "The Ballooning Costs of Long-Term Care."
https://www.americanactionforum.org/research/the-ballooning-costs-of-long-term-care

underestimated, especially by those who have maintained robust health and find it difficult to envision future declines to their condition.

Another piece of planning for long-term care costs is anticipating inflation. It's common knowledge that prices have been and keep rising, which will lower your purchasing power on everything from food to medical care. Long-term care is a big piece of the inflation-disparity pie, which is part of why many find their estimates of nursing home care widely miss the mark. According to one survey, people expected to pay around $25,350 in annual out-of-pocket long-term care expenses, but, in reality, they'll more likely pay over $47,000.[9]

While local costs vary from state to state, here's the national median for various forms of long-term care (plus projections that account for a 3 percent annual inflation, so you can see what we are referencing):[10]

---

[9] Moll Law Group. 2021. "The Cost of Long-Term Care." https://www.molllawgroup.com/the-cost-of-long-term-care.html
[10] Genworth Financial. January 2022. "Cost of Care Survey 2021." https://www.genworth.com/aging-and-you/finances/cost-of-care.html

Long-Term Care Costs: Inflation				
	Home Health Care, Homemaker Services	Adult Day Care	Assisted Living	Nursing Home (semi-private room)
Annual 2021	$59,488	$20,280	$54,000	$94,900
Annual 2031	$79,947	$27,255	$72,571	$127,538
Annual 2041	$107,442	$36,628	$97,530	$171,400
Annual 2051	$144,393	$49,225	$131,072	$230,347

Fund Your Long-Term Care

One critical mistake we see are those who haven't planned for long-term care because they assume the government will provide everything. But that's a big misconception. The government has two health insurance programs: Medicare and Medicaid. These can greatly assist you in your health care needs in retirement but usually don't provide enough coverage to cover all your health care costs in retirement. Our firm isn't a government outpost, so we don't get to make decisions when it comes to forming policy and specifics about either one of these programs. We're going to give the overview of both, but if you want to dive into the details of these programs, you can visit www.Medicare.gov and www.Medicaid.gov.

Medicare
Medicare covers those aged sixty-five and older and those who are disabled. Medicare's coverage of any nursing-home-related

health issues is limited. It might cover your nursing home stay if it is not a "custodial" stay, and it isn't long-term. For example, if you break a bone or suffer a stroke, stay in a nursing home for rehabilitative care, and then return home, Medicare may cover you. But, if you have developed dementia or are looking to move to a nursing facility because you can no longer bathe, dress, toilet, feed yourself, or take care of your hygiene, etc., then Medicare is not going to pay for your nursing home costs.[11]

You can enroll in Medicare anytime during the three months before and four months after your sixty-fifth birthday. Miss your enrollment deadline, and you could risk paying increased premiums for the rest of your life. On top of prompt enrollment, there are a few other things to think about when it comes to Medicare, not least among them being the need to understand the different "parts," what they do, and what they don't cover.

Part A

Medicare Part A is what you might think of as "classic" Medicare. Hospital care, some types of home health care, and major medical care fall under this. While most enrollees pay nothing for this service (as they likely paid into the system for at least ten years), you may end up paying, either based on work history or delayed signup. In 2022, the highest premium is $499 per month, and a hospital stay does have a deductible, $1,556.[12] And, if you have a hospital stay that surpasses sixty days, you could be looking at additional costs; keep in mind, Medicare doesn't pay for long-term care and services.

---

[11] Medicare.gov. "What Part A covers." https://www.medicare.gov/what-medicare-covers/part-a/what-part-a-covers.html

[12] Medicare. "Medicare 2022 Costs at a Glance." https://www.medicare.gov/your-medicare-costs/medicare-costs-at-a-glance

Part B

Medicare Part B is an essential piece of wrap-around coverage for Medicare Part A. It helps pay for doctor visits and outpatient services. This also comes with a price tag: Although the Part B deductible is only $233 in 2022, you will still pay 20 percent of all costs after that, with no limit on out-of-pocket expenses.[13]

Part C

Medicare Part C, more commonly known as Medicare Advantage plans, are an alternative to a combination of Parts A, B, and sometimes D. Administered through private insurance companies, these have a variety of costs and restrictions, and they are subject to the specific policies and rules of the issuing carrier.

Part D

Medicare Part D is also through a private insurer and is supplemental to Parts A and B, as its primary purpose is to cover prescription drugs. Like any private insurance plan, Part D has its quirks and rules that vary from insurer to insurer.

The Donut Hole

Even with a "Part D" in place, you may still have a coverage gap between what your Part D private drug insurance pays for your prescription and what basic Medicare pays. In 2022, the coverage gap is $4,430, meaning, after you meet your private prescription insurance limit, you will spend no more than 25 percent of your drug costs out-of-pocket before Medicare will kick in to pay for more prescription drugs.[14]

---

[13] Ibid.
[14] Medicare. "Costs in the coverage gap."
https://www.medicare.gov/drug-coverage-part-d/costs-for-medicare-drug-coverage/costs-in-the-coverage-gap

Medicare Supplements

Medicare Supplement Insurance, MedSup, Medigap, or plans labeled Medicare Part F, G, H, I, J . . . Known by a variety of monikers, this is just a fancy way of saying "medical coverage for those over sixty-five that picks up the tab for whatever the federal Medicare program(s) doesn't." Again, costs, limitations, etc., vary by carrier.

Does that sound like a bunch of government alphabet soup to you? It certainly does to us. And, did you read the fine print? Unpredictable costs, varied restrictions, difficult-to-compare benefits, donut holes, and coverage gaps. That's par for the course with health care plans through the course of our adult lives. What gives? We thought Medicare was supposed to be easier, comprehensive, and at no cost!

The truth is there is no stage of life when health care is easy to understand.

Most people don't realize Medicare has no coverage for intermediate or long-term care. Medicare only covers you for skilled care (you can recover). There is a huge gap in the Medicare system in the form of long-term care.

For many people, it's not a matter of if, but when a long-term care stay will become necessary. When this happens, it's too late to plan for it. We can't plan for things after the fact.

The best thing you can do for yourself is to scope out the health care field early, compare costs often, and prepare for out-of-pocket costs well in advance—decades, if possible.

Medicaid

Medicaid is a program the states administer, so funding, protocol, and limitations vary. Compared to Medicare, Medicaid more widely covers nursing home care, but it targets a different demographic: those with low incomes.

If you have more assets than the Medicaid limit in your state and need nursing home care, you will need to use those assets to pay for your care. You will also have a list of additional state-approved ways to spend some of these assets over the Medicaid limit, such as pre-purchasing burial plots and funeral expenses or paying off debts. After that, your remaining assets fund your nursing home stay until they are gone, at which point Medicaid will jump in.

Some people aren't stymied by this, thinking they will just pass on their financial assets early, gifting them to relatives, friends, and causes so they can qualify for Medicaid when they need it. However, to prevent this exact scenario, Uncle Sam has implemented the look-back period. Currently, if you enroll in Medicaid, you are subject to having the government scrutinize the last five years of your finances for large gifts or expenses that may subject you to penalties, temporarily making you ineligible for Medicaid coverage.

So, if you're planning to preserve your money for future generations and retain control of your financial resources during your lifetime, you'll probably want to prepare for the costs of longevity beyond a "government plan."

Self-Funding

One way to fund a longer life is the old-fashioned way, through self-funding. There are a variety of financial tools you can use, and they all have their pros and cons. If your assets are in low-interest financial vehicles (savings, bonds, CDs), you risk letting inflation erode the value of your dollar. Or, if you are relying on the stock market, you have more growth potential, but you'll also want to consider the possible implications of market volatility. What if your assets take a hit? If you suffer a loss in your retirement portfolio in early or mid-retirement, you might have the option to "tighten your belt," so to speak, and cut back on discretionary spending to allow your portfolio the room to bounce back. But, if you are retired and depend on income from a stock account that just hit a downward stride, what are you going to do?

HSAs

These days, you might also be able to self-fund through a health savings account, or HSA, if you have access to one through a high-deductible health plan (you will not qualify to save in an HSA after enrolling in Medicare). In an HSA, any growth of your tax-deductible contributions will be tax-free, and any distributions paid out for qualified health costs are also tax-free. Long-term care expenses count as health costs, so, if this is an option available to you, it is one way to use the tax advantages to self-fund your longevity. Bear in mind, if you are younger than sixty-five, any money you use for nonqualified expenses will be subject to taxes and penalties, and, if you are older than sixty-five, any HSA money you use for non-medical expenses is subject to income tax.

LTCI

One slightly more nuanced way to pay for longevity, specifically for long-term care, is long-term care insurance, or LTCI. As car insurance protects your assets in case of a car accident and home insurance protects your assets in case something happens to your house, long-term care insurance aims to protect your assets in case you need long-term care in an at-home or nursing home situation.

As with other types of insurance, you will pay a monthly or annual premium in exchange for an insurance company paying for long-term care down the road. Typically, policies cover two to three years of care, which is adequate for an "average" situation: it's estimated 70 percent of Americans will need about three years of long-term care of some kind. However, it's important to consider you might not be "average" when you are preparing for long-term care costs; on average, 20 percent of today's sixty-five-year-olds could need care for longer than five years.[15]

---

[15] LongTermCare.gov. February 18, 2020. "How Much Care Will You Need?" https://acl.gov/ltc/basic-needs/how-much-care-will-you-need

Now, there are a few oft-cited components of LTCI that make it unattractive for some:

- Expense — LTCI can be expensive. It is generally less expensive the younger you are, but a fifty-five-year-old couple who purchased LTCI in 2022 could expect to pay $2,080 each year for an average three-year coverage policy. And the annual cost only increases from there the older you are.[16]
- Limited options — Let's face it: LTCI may be expensive for consumers, but it can also be expensive for companies that offer it. With fewer companies willing to take on that expense, this narrows the market, meaning opportunities to price shop for policies with different options or custom benefits are limited.
- If you know you need it, you might not be able to get it — Insurance companies offering LTCI are taking on a risk that you may need LTCI. That risk is the foundation of the product—you may or may not need it. If you know you will need it because you have a dementia diagnosis or another illness for which you will need long-term care, you will likely not qualify for LTCI coverage.
- Use it or lose it — If you have LTCI and are in the minority of Americans who die having never needed long-term care, all the money you paid into your LTCI policy is gone.
- Possibly fluctuating rates — Your rate is not locked in on LTCI. Companies maintain the ability to raise or lower your premium amounts. This means some seniors face an ultimatum: Keep funding a policy at what might be a less affordable rate *or* lose coverage and let go of all the money they paid in so far.

---

[16] American Association for Long-Term Care Insurance. January 12, 2022. "2022 National Long-Term Care Insurance Price Index." https://www.aaltci.org/long-term-care-insurance/learning-center/ltcfacts-2022.php

After that, you might be thinking, "How can people possibly be interested in LTCI?" But let us repeat ourselves—as many as 70 percent of Americans will need long-term care. And, although only 8 percent of Americans have purchased LTCI, keep in mind the high cost of nursing home care. Can you afford $7,000 a month to put into nursing home care and still have enough left over to protect your legacy? It is vitally important to have a plan in place to deal with longevity and long-term care if you intend to leave a financial legacy.

At Capital A, part of our process focuses on healthcare planning. The reason we talk about LTCI is because there are some gaps in Medicare that do not cover extended healthcare costs. Long-term care insurance can be a great way cover yourself and protect your hard-earned assets from a nursing home stay. The biggest problem we see retirees facing is when one spouse goes into a nursing home and spends down the majority of the assets, leaving the surviving spouse with nothing. To prevent this issue, we always look ahead to potential healthcare expenses in retirement, not only for Medicare, but for the gaps in Medicare that can be detrimental to a successful retirement.

There are plenty of ways to pay and plan for LTC expenses, but we often recommend our clients pay for this through a combo LTC/life insurance policy, when appropriate. This policy is one where you purchase life insurance, but also have LTC benefits in the form of a rider. So, let's look at an example.

Let's say someone named Ron (a hypothetical person) purchases a life insurance policy with a $500,000 death benefit. This death benefit can be accessed two ways. The first, if he does need assistance from an LTC facility's in-home healthcare, he can access a small percentage of his death benefit per month tax free. For instance, he might access $10,000/month tax-free to help pay for these LTC expenses. The second way is that, if he doesn't need this money for LTC expenses, his $500,000 death benefit would pass to his named beneficiaries tax-free, assuming he keeps the policy in force. So, someone is getting this benefit: Either Ron for his LTC expenses, or his beneficiaries in the form of a tax-free death benefit.

As a side note: this strategy is not beneficial for everyone and it does involve medical underwriting. But, if you can qualify and the premium is affordable for you, a hybrid life insurance policy may be a good way to help protect yourself from these LTC expenses in retirement.

A few relevant statistics to keep in mind:
- The longer you live, the more likely you are to continue living; the longer you live, the more health care you will likely need to pay for.
- The median cost of a private nursing home room in the United States in 2021 was $9,034 a month.[17] But keep in mind, that is just the nursing home—it doesn't include other medical costs, let alone pleasantries, like entertainment or hobby spending.
- In 2021, Fidelity calculated that a healthy couple retiring at age sixty-five could expect to pay around $300,000 over the course of retirement to cover health and medical expenses.
- They estimate that the average man will need $143,000, and the average woman needs about 10 percent more, or $157,000, because of women's longer life expectancies.[18]

We know. Whoa, there, Dave and Brandon, I was hoping to have a realistic idea of health costs, not be driven over by a cement mixer!

---

[17] Genworth Financial. January 31, 2022. "Genworth 2020 Cost of Care Survey." https://www.genworth.com/aging-and-you/finances/cost-of-care.html

[18] Elizabeth O'Brien. Money. May 10, 2021. "Health Care Now Costs Couples $300,000 in Retirement, According to Fidelity's Latest Estimate." https://money.com/health-care-costs-retirement-fidelity-2021-study/. The $300,000 estimate assumes an opposite-gender couple, where the man lives until age eighty-seven and the woman until age eighty-nine.

The good news is, while we don't know these exact costs in advance, we know there *will* be costs. And you won't have to pay your total Medicare lifetime premiums in one day as a lump sum. Now that you have a good idea of health care costs in retirement, you can *plan* for them! That's the real point, here: Planning in advance can keep you from feeling nickel-and-dimed to your wits' end. Instead, having a sizeable portion of your assets earmarked for health care can allow you the freedom to choose health care networks, coverage options, and long-term care possibilities you like and that you think offer you the best in life.

Product Riders

LTCI and self-funding are not the only ways to plan for the expenses of longevity. Some companies are getting creative with their products, particularly insurance companies. One way they are retooling to meet people's needs is through optional product riders on annuities and life insurance. Elsewhere in this book, we talk about annuity basics, but here's a brief overview: Annuities are insurance contracts. You pay the insurance company a premium, either as a lump sum or as a series of payments over a set amount of time, in exchange for guaranteed income payments. One of the advantages of an annuity is it has access to riders, which allow you to tweak your contract for a fee, usually about 1 percent of the contract value annually. One annuity rider some companies offer is a long-term care rider. If you have an annuity with a long-term care rider and are not in need of long-term care, your contract behaves as any annuity contract would—nothing changes. Generally speaking, if you reach a point when you can't perform multiple functions of daily life on your own, you notify the insurance company, and a representative will turn on those provisions of your contract.

Like LTCI, different companies and products offer different options. Some annuity long-term care riders offer coverage of two years in a nursing home situation. Others cap expenses at two times the original annuity's value. It greatly depends. Some people prefer this option because there isn't a "use-it-or-lose-it" piece; if you die without ever having needed long-term care, you still will have had the income benefit from the base contract. Still, as with any annuities or insurance contracts, there are the usual restrictions and limitations. Withdrawing money from the contract will affect future income payments, early distributions can result in a penalty, income taxes may apply, and, because the insurance company's solvency is what guarantees your payments, it's important to do your research about the insurance company you are considering purchasing a contract from.

Understandably, a discussion on long-term care is bound to feel at least a little tedious. Yet, this is a critical piece of planning for income in retirement, particularly if you want to leave a legacy.

We had a woman named Gloria come to us for our first appointment strategy session, and we started asking her about her retirement. Like most people, she was concerned about outliving her money and having an income plan, but she then started to explain the dynamic of her family and what she had gone through. We found out through conversation that her mother was in a nursing home for over ten years with Alzheimer's. They had no plan to cover an LTC stay so her hard-working parents and father had to spend down all of their assets over that time until her mother went on to state pay program through Medicaid. This was devasting for her father, and for Gloria, who was the primary caretaker.

Upon the passing of her beloved mother, Gloria's father had to sell the house and move in with her and her husband. Her father is now ninety-five years old, and Gloria has once again become a primary caregiver. Gloria is a wonderful person, but she's not a nurse. Unfortunately, this caregiving is significantly impacting her retirement as she is unable to do the things she wanted to do during this time.

Spousal Planning

Here's one thing to keep in mind no matter how you plan to save: Many of us will be planning for more than ourselves. Look back at all the stats on health events and the likelihood of long life and long-term care. If they hold true for a single individual, then the likelihood of having a costly health or long-term care event is even higher for a married couple. You'll be planning for not just one life, but two. So, when it comes to long-term care insurance, annuities, self-funding, or whatever strategy you are looking at using, be sure you are funding longevity for the both of you.

CHAPTER 2

Taxes

Where to begin with taxes? Perhaps by acknowledging we all bear responsibility for the resources we share. Roads, bridges, schools . . . It is the patriotic duty of every American to pay their fair share of taxes. Many would agree with us, though, while they don't mind paying their fair share, they're not interested in paying one cent more than that!

Now, just talking taxes probably takes your mind to April—tax season. You are probably thinking about all the forms you collect and how you file. Perhaps you are thinking about your certified public accountant or another qualified tax professional and saying to yourself, "I've already got taxes taken care of, thanks!"

However, what we see when people come into our office is that their relationship with their tax professional is purely a January through April relationship. That means they may have a tax professional, but not a tax *planner*.

What we mean is tax planning extends beyond filing taxes. In April, we are required to settle our accounts with the IRS to make sure we have paid up on our bill or to even the score if we have overpaid. But real tax planning is about making each financial move in a way that allows you to keep the most money in your pocket and out of Uncle Sam's.

Now, as a caveat, we want to emphasize we are neither CPAs nor tax planners, but we see the way taxes affect our clients, and we have plenty of experience helping clients implement tax-efficient strategies in their retirement plans in conjunction with their tax professionals.

It is especially important to us to help our clients develop tax-efficient strategies in their retirement plans because each dollar they can keep in their pockets is a dollar we can put to work.

We find that a lot of people have no idea what their projected tax liability is in retirement until they come and meet with us. Even people who are great at saving sometimes just don't realize the consequences taxes can have on their retirement.

One couple, who we'll call Charlie and Betty, both had very good Social Security, pretty large pensions, and every dollar they had saved was in an IRA—about $2 million. They didn't understand the possible ramifications of those accounts, things like the required minimum distributions that begin at age seventy-two and the future tax liabilities.

Sometimes people like Charlie and Betty, who can anticipate Social Security and pension payouts, already have more than enough income to retire. That's a great situation to be in! But this situation also means their taxes in retirement could bump them up a tax bracket or two.

Through tax planning before their retirement, we could look at converting IRAs to other vehicles to help minimize the overall tax burden. Roth IRAs can be great for this kind of situation. A life insurance policy that has a tax-free death benefit can be as well, allowing more of their money to be passed on to the policyholder's children.

When we meet with clients, we use software that generates a report showing the possible effects of a conversion from a traditional IRA to a Roth IRA. Here's a hypothetical example. The values on the following page are based on what we believe are reasonable forward-looking assumptions.

CAPITALIZE ON RETIREMENT | 23

Current Account Value	**$1,150,000**
Assumed Tax Liability	**24% all years**
Annual Pre-Tax Earnings Rate Based on 71/29 split of equities and fixed income, with equities earning 6% fixed income earning 2.5%	**4.99%**
Assumed Account Expenses	1%

The values below show two scenarios:

(1) The total taxes paid if you live to age 90, assuming you continue to keep your qualified account, take RMDs when required, and reinvest these RMDs in a taxable account

(2) The total taxes paid if you live to age 90, assuming you roll over your qualified account to a Roth account today

Keep Qualified Account		Convert to Roth	
Total taxes paid on RMDs at time of withdrawals	$441,131	Taxes paid on conversion	$276,000
Taxes paid on reinvested RMDs	$198,082	Taxes paid on Roth account growth	$0
Taxes paid on remaining account value at death	$307,192	Taxes paid on remaining Roth account value at death:	$0
TOTAL TAXES PAID: $946,405		**$276,000**	

(This hypothetical example is not guaranteed and does not reflect any specific product or investment. This example assumes a couple, both age sixty, keeps the qualified account until age seventy-two, and the clients live to age ninety. Tax-free income is available from the Roth after age fifty nine and a half, and the account has been open for at least five years.)

The Fed

Now, in the United States, taxes can be a rather uncertain proposition. Depending on who is in the White House and which party controls Congress, we might be tempted to assume tax rates could either decline or increase in the next four to eight years accordingly. However, there is one (large!) factor we, as a nation, must confront: the national debt.

Currently, according to USDebtClock.org, we are over $29,000,000,000,000 in debt and climbing. That's $29.0 *trillion* with a "T." With just $1 trillion, you could park it in the bank at a zero percent interest rate and spend more than $54 million every day for fifty years without hitting a zero balance.

Even if Congress got a handle and stopped that debt from its daily compound, divided by each taxpayer, we each would owe about $214,000. So, will that be check or cash?

Our point here isn't to give you anxiety. We're just cautioning you that even with the rosiest of outlooks on our personal income tax rates, none of us should count on low tax rates for the long term. Instead, you and your network of professionals (tax, legal, and financial) should constantly be looking for ways to take advantage of tax-saving opportunities as they come. After all, the best "luck" is when proper planning meets opportunity.

So, how can we get started?

Know Your Limits

One of the foundational pieces of tax planning is knowing what tax bracket you are in, based on your income after subtracting pre-tax or untaxed assets. Your income taxes are based on your taxable income.

One reason to know your taxable income and your income tax rate is so you can see how far away you are from the next lower or higher tax bracket. This is particularly important when it comes to decisions such as gifting and Roth IRA rollovers.

For instance, based on the 2022 tax table, Mallory and Ralph's taxable income is just over $345,000, putting them in the 32 percent tax bracket and about $4,900 above the upper end of the 24 percent tax bracket. They have already maxed out their retirement funds' tax-exempt contributions for the year. Their daughter, Stephanie, is a sophomore in college. This couple could shave a considerable amount off their tax bill if they use the $4,900 to help Stephanie out with groceries and school—something they were likely to do, anyway, but now can deliberately be put to work for them in their overall financial strategy.

Now, we use Mallory and Ralph only as an example—your circumstances are probably different—but we think this nicely illustrates the way planning ahead for taxes can save you money.

Assuming a Lower Tax Rate

Many people anticipate being in a lower tax bracket in retirement. It makes sense: You won't be contributing to retirement funds; you'll be drawing from them. And you won't have all those work expenses—work clothes, transportation, lunch meetings, etc.

Yet, do you really plan on changing your lifestyle after retirement? Do you plan to cut down on the number of times you eat out, scale back vacations, and skimp on travel?

What we see in our office is many couples spend more in the first few years, or maybe the first decade, of retirement. Sure, that may taper off later on, but usually only just in time for their budget to be hit with greater health and long-term care expenses. Do you see where this is going? Many people plan as though their taxable income will be lower in retirement and are surprised when the tax bills come in and look more or less the same as they used to. It's better to plan for the worst and hope for the best, wouldn't you agree?

401(k)/IRA

One sometimes-unexpected piece of tax planning in retirement concerns your 401(k) or IRA. Most of us have one of these accounts or an equivalent. Throughout our working lives, we pay in, dutifully socking away a portion of our earnings in these tax-deferred accounts. There's the rub: tax-deferred. Not tax-free. Very rarely is anything free of taxation when you get down to it. Using 401(k)s and IRAs in retirement is no different. The taxes the government deferred when you were in your working years are now coming due, and you will pay taxes on that income at whatever your current tax rate is.

Just to ensure Uncle Sam gets his due, the government also has a required minimum distribution, or RMD, rule. Beginning at age seventy-two, you are required to withdraw a certain minimum amount every year from your 401(k) or IRA, or else you will face a 50 percent tax penalty on any RMD monies you should have withdrawn but didn't—and that's on top of income tax.

Of course, there is also the Roth IRA. You can think of the difference between a Roth IRA and a traditional retirement account as the difference between taxing the seed and taxing the harvest. Because Roth IRAs are funded with post-tax dollars, there aren't tax penalties for early withdrawals of the principal nor are there taxes on the growth after you reach age fifty-nine-and-one-half. Perhaps best of all, there are no RMDs. Of course, you must own a Roth IRA for a minimum of five years before you are able to take advantage of all its features.

This is one more area where it pays to be aware of your tax bracket. Some people may find it advantageous to "convert" their traditional retirement account funds to Roth account funds in a year during which they are in a lower tax bracket. Others may opt to put any excess RMDs from their traditional retirement accounts into other products, like stocks or insurance.

Does that make your head spin? Understandable. That's why it's so important to work with a financial professional and tax planner who can help you not only execute these sorts of tax-efficient strategies but also help you understand what you are doing and why.

CHAPTER 3

Market Volatility

Up and down. Roller coaster. Merry-go-round. Bulls and bears. Peak-to-trough.

Sound familiar? This is the language we use to talk about the stock market. With volatility and spikes, even our language is jarring, bracing, and vivid.

Still, financial strategies tend to revolve around market-based products, for good reasons. For one thing, there is no other financial class that packs the same potential for growth, pound for pound, as stock-based products. Because of growth potential, inflation protection, and new opportunities, it may be unwise to avoid the market entirely.

However, along with the potential for growth is the potential for loss. Many of the people we see in our office come in still feeling a bit burned from the market drama of 2000 to 2010. That was a rough stretch, and many of us are once-bitten-twice-shy investors, right?

So how do we balance these factors? How do we try to satisfy both the need for protection and the need for growth?

For one thing, it is important to recognize the value of diversity. Now, we're not just talking about the diversity of assets among different kinds of stocks, or even different kinds of stocks and bonds. That's only one kind of diversity; while important, both stocks and bonds, though different, are both still market-based products. Most market-based products, even within a diverse portfolio, tend to rise or lower as a whole, just like an incoming tide. Therefore, a portfolio diverse in only market-sourced products won't automatically protect your assets during times when the market declines.

In addition to the sort of "horizontal diversity" you have by purchasing a variety of stocks and bonds from different companies, we also suggest you think about "vertical diversity," or diversity among asset classes. This means having different product types, including securities products, bank products, and insurance products—with varying levels of growth potential, liquidity, and protection—all in accordance with your unique situation, goals, and needs.

Our process for determining a client's risk tolerance is very different than many advisors. We don't simply ask our clients how they feel toward risk in the markets, leading to general, less helpful answers like "aggressive" or "conservative." We use a software that gives us more detailed insight into how our clients feel toward risk. Our process is more comprehensive.

Some of the program's questions involve choosing different financial scenarios to determine specific risk-assessment preferences, such as:

Would you rather:

Option A: Flip a coin and have a 50/50 chance of your portfolio gaining 100 percent if it's heads or losing 50 percent if it's tails.

Option B: Earn 5 percent.

This is just an example, but at the end of the questionnaire, the software calculates a risk score, anywhere from 1 to 99. A score of 1 would mean you are ultra-conservative and can't stomach any risk at all. A score of 99 would mean you are ultra-aggressive and seeking maximum growth.

Our clients typically fall into the 35 to 55 range. They are nearing retirement and they don't want a down market determining if they can retire or not. Therefore, they take some risk off of the table. They are looking for protected rates of return and not tons of volatility.

We believe this software is a good approach to establish a baseline, but at Capital A, we also understand there's more nuance to creating a customized retirement strategy than simply using software or clarifying general risk terms.

We believe your money should be divided into three buckets: protection, income, and growth.

The protection bucket is for those unexpected moments that arise in life, the emergencies we all encounter.

The income bucket is for financing your general lifestyle and monthly bills. For example, using some of your retirement savings to purchase an annuity, such as a fixed index annuity, that could provide a consistent, monthly income stream, would fall within this category.

Finally, the growth bucket is where you can be more aggressive with your investments in the market since you already have your protection and income buckets accounted for. This bucket is subject to more volatility and market risk. You could lose money, but you also have the potential for higher gains and the opportunity to help combat inflation with these funds.

Figuring out your protection and income buckets can help us determine how much risk you're comfortable taking in the markets, if any at all. Remember, your essential daily income shouldn't depend on the markets, it should depend on math!

The Color of Money

When you're looking at the overall diversity of your portfolio, part of the equation is knowing which products fit in what category: what has liquidity, what has protection, and what has growth potential.

Before we dive in, keep in mind these aren't absolutes. You might think of liquidity, growth, and protection as primary colors. While some products will look pretty much yellow, red, or blue, others will have a mix of characteristics, making them more green, orange, or purple.

Growth

We like to think of the growth category as red. It's powerful, it's somewhat volatile, and it's also the category where there are the greatest opportunities for growth and loss. Often, products in the growth category will have a good deal of liquidity but very little protection. These are our market-based products and strategies, and we think of them mostly in shades of red and orange, to designate their growth and liquidity. This is a good place to be when you're young—think fast cars and flashy leather jackets—but its allure often wanes as you move closer to retirement. Examples of "red" products include:

- Stocks
- Equities
- Exchange-traded funds
- Mutual funds
- Corporate bonds
- Real estate investment trusts
- Speculations
- Alternative investments

Liquidity

Yellow is our liquid category color. We typically recommend having at least enough yellow money to cover six months' to a year's worth of expenses in case of emergency. Yellow assets don't need a lot of growth potential; they just need to be readily available when we need them. The "yellow" category includes assets like:

- Cash
- Money market accounts

Protection

The color of protection, to us, is blue. Tranquil, peaceful, sure, even if it lacks a certain amount of flash. This is the direction we like to see people generally move toward as they're nearing retirement. The red, flashy look of stock market returns and the risk of possible overnight losses is less attractive as we near retirement and look for more consistency and reliability. While the protection category doesn't come with a lot of liquidity, the products here are backed by an insurance company, a bank, or a government entity. "Blue" products include things such as:

- Certificates of deposit (backed by banks)
- Government-based bonds (backed by the U.S. government)
- Life insurance (backed by insurance companies)
- Annuities (backed by insurance companies)

401(k)s

We want to take a second to specifically address the products many retirees will be using to build their retirement income: the 401(k) and other retirement accounts. Any of these retirement accounts (IRAs, 401(k)s, 403(b)s, etc.) are basically "tax wrappers." What do we mean by that? Well, depending on your plan provider, a 401(k) could include target-date funds, passively managed products, stocks, bonds, mutual funds, or even variable, fixed, and fixed index annuities, all collected in one place and governed by rules (a.k.a. the "tax wrapper"). These rules govern how much money you can put inside, what ways you can put it in, when you will pay taxes on it, and when you can take the money out. Inside the 401(k), each of the products inside the "tax wrapper" might have its own fees or commissions, in addition to the management fee you pay on the 401(k) itself.

Dollar-Cost Averaging

With 401(k)s and other market-based retirement products, when you are investing for the long term, dollar-cost averaging is a concept that can work in your favor. When the market is trending up, if you are consistently paying in money, month over month, great; your investments can grow, and you are adding to your assets. When the market takes a dip, no problem; your dollars buy more shares at a lower price. At some point, we hope the market will rebound, in which case your shares can grow and possibly be more valuable than they were before. This concept is what we call "dollar-cost averaging." While it can't ensure a profit or guarantee against losses, it's a time-tested strategy for investing in a volatile market.

However, when you are in retirement, this strategy may work against you. You may have heard of "reverse" dollar-cost averaging. Before, when the market lost ground, you were "bargain-shopping"; your dollars purchased more assets at a reduced price. When you are in retirement, you are no longer the purchaser; you are selling. So, in a down market, you have to sell more assets to make the same amount of money as what you made in a favorable market.

We've had lots of people step into our office to talk to us about this, emphasizing, "my advisor says the market always bounces back, and I have to just hold on for the long term."

There's some basis for this thinking; thus far, the market has always rebounded to higher heights than before. But this is no guarantee, and the prospect of potentially higher returns in five years may not be very helpful in retirement if you are relying on the income from those returns to pay this month's electric bill, for example.

Is There a "Perfect" Product?

To bring us back around to the discussion of protection, growth, and liquidity, the ideal product would be a "ten" in all three categories, right? Completely guaranteed, doubling in size every few years, and accessible whenever you want. Does such a product exist? Anyone who says "yes" is either ignorant or malevolent.

Instead of running in circles looking for that perfect product, the silver bullet, the unicorn of financial strategies, it's more important to circle back to the concept of a balanced, asset-diverse portfolio.

This is why your interests may be best served when you work with a trusted financial professional who knows what various financial products can do and how to use them in your personal retirement strategy.

CHAPTER 4

Retirement Income

Retirement. For many of us, it's what we've saved for and dreamed of, pinning our hopes to a magical someday. Is that someday full of traveling? Is it filled with grandkids? Gardening? Maybe your fondest dream is simply never having to work again, never having to clock in or be accountable to someone else.

Your ability to do these things all hinges on *income*. Without the money to support these dreams, even a basic level of work-free lifestyle is unsustainable. That's why planning for your income in retirement is so foundational. But where do we begin?

It's easy to feel overwhelmed by this question. Some may feel the urge to amass a large lump sum and then try to put it all in one product—insurance, investments, liquid assets—to provide all the growth, liquidity, and income they need. Instead, we think you need a more balanced approach. After all, retirement planning isn't magic. Like we mention elsewhere, there is no single product that can be all things to all people (or even all things to one person). No approach works unilaterally for everyone. That's why it's important to talk to a financial professional who can help you lay down the basics and take you step-by-step through the process. Not only will you have the assurance you have addressed the areas you need to, but you will also have an ally who can help you break down the process and help keep you from feeling overwhelmed.

Sources of Income

Thinking of all the pieces of your retirement expenses might be intimidating. Once you have laid everything out, you can begin to sort things into categories.

Once you have a good overall picture of where your expenses will lie, you can start stacking up the resources to cover them.

Social Security

Social Security is a guaranteed, inflation-protected federal insurance program playing a significant part in most of our retirement plans. From delaying until you've reached full retirement age or beyond to examining spousal benefits, as we discuss elsewhere in this book, there is plenty you can do to try to make the most of this monthly benefit. As with all your retirement income sources, it's important to consider how to make this resource stretch to provide the most bang and buck for your situation.

Pension

Another generally reliable source of retirement income for you might be a pension, if you are one of the lucky people who still has one.

If you don't have a pension, go ahead and skim on to the next section. If you do have a pension, keep on reading.

Because your pension can be such a central piece of your retirement income plan, you will want to put some thought into answering basic questions about it.

How well is your pension funded? Since the heyday of the pension plan, many companies and governments have neglected to adequately fund their pension obligations, causing a persistent problem with this otherwise reliable asset. However, research conducted by the Pew Charitable Trusts showed a collective increase in assets exceeding half a trillion dollars in state retirement plans fueled by strong market investment returns in fiscal 2021. Pew's estimates that state retirement systems rose to 80 percent funding for the first time in 2008.[19]

Consider the factors at play, though. Pensions had been underfunded and gained a boost from strong market performance in 2021. What happens to the solvency of those pension funds if the market declines?

It can be worthwhile to keep tabs on your pension's health and know what your options are for withdrawing your pension. If you have already retired and made those decisions, this may be a foregone conclusion. If not, it pays to know what you can expect and what decisions you can make, such as taking spousal options to cover your husband or wife if he or she outlives you.

Also, some companies are incentivizing lump-sum payouts of pensions to reduce the companies' payment liabilities. If that's the case with your employer, talk to your financial professional to see if it might be prudent to do something like that or if it might be better to stick with lifetime payments or other options.

Your 401(k) and IRA

One "modern way" to save for retirement is in a 401(k) or IRA (or their nonprofit or governmental equivalents). These tax-advantaged accounts are, in our opinion, a poor substitute for pensions, but one of the biggest disservices we do to ourselves is to not take full advantage of them in the first place. According to one article, only 41 percent of Americans invest in a 401(k),

---

[19] pewtrusts.org. September 14, 2021. "The State Pension Funding Gap: Plans Have Stabilized in Wake of Pandemic"
https://www.pewtrusts.org/en/research-and-analysis/issue-briefs/2021/09/the-state-pension-funding-gap-plans-have-stabilized-in-wake-of-pandemic

though 68 percent of employed Americans have access to a 401(k) benefit option.[20]

Also, if you have changed jobs over the years, do the work of tracking down any benefits from your past employers. You might have an IRA here or a 401(k) there; keep track of those so you can pull them together and look at those assets when you're ready to look at establishing sources of retirement income.

Do You Have...

- Life insurance?
- Annuities?
- Long-term care insurance?
- Any passive income sources?
- Stock and bond portfolios?
- Liquid assets? (What's in your bank account?)
- Alternative investments?
- Rental properties?

It's important, if you are going through the work of sitting with a financial professional, to look at your full retirement income picture and pull together *all* your assets, no matter how big or small. From the free insurance policy offered at your bank to the sizable investment in your brother-in-law's modestly successful furniture store, you want to have a good idea of where your money is.

We sometimes compare this experience to going through the junk drawer at home. Over the years, you may have thrown a roll of tape in there, a spare set of keys, or a gift card to your favorite restaurant. At first, you may have a general idea of what the junk drawer contains, but over time, you forget what all is in there.

---

[20] Amin Dabit. personalcapital.com. April 1, 2021. "The Average 401k Balance by Age." https://www.personalcapital.com/blog/retirement-planning/average-401k-balance-age

Most people know they need to invest in some form or another throughout their careers, so they establish a "junk drawer" of savings. Between 401(k) plans at current and past employers, small stock purchases, and life insurance policies, by the time retirement rolls around, it's hard to remember where all they've scattered their various savings.

When you meet with us, we'll take a comprehensive look at every investment you've made over the years and help ensure everything works together in a cohesive fashion.

Retirement Income Needs

How much income will you need in retirement? How do you determine that? A lot of people work toward a random number, thinking, "If I can just have a million dollars, I'll be comfortable in retirement!" Don't get us wrong; it is possible to save up a lot of money and then retire in the hopes you can keep your monthly expenses lower than some set estimation. But we think this carries a general risk of running out of money. Instead, we work with our clients to find out what their current and projected income needs are and then work from there to see how we might cover any gaps between what they have and what they want.

Goals and Dreams

It's not uncommon for Americans to spend more time planning our vacations than we spend planning our retirements. Maybe it's because planning a vacation is less stressful: Having a week at the beach go awry is, well, a walk on the beach compared to running out of money in retirement. Whatever the case, perhaps it would be better if you thought of your retirement as a vacation in and of itself—no clocking in, no boss, no overtime. If you felt unlimited by financial strain, what would you do?

Would an endless vacation for you mean Paris and Rome? Would it mean mentoring at children's clubs or serving at the local soup kitchen? Or maybe it would mean deepening your ties to those immediately around you—neighbors, friends, and family. Maybe it would mean more time to take part in the hobbies and activities you love. Have you been considering a second (or even third) act as a small-business owner, turning a hobby or passion into a revenue source?

This is your time to daydream and answer the question: If you could do anything, what would you do?

After that, it's a matter of putting a dollar amount on it. What are the costs of round-the-world travel? One couple we know said their highest priority was to retire at age sixty and take their kids on frequent vacations. They both started working at a young age and didn't grow up with much money, so they didn't take many trips as children.

To make up for this, they wanted to receive about $30,000 each year as a travel fund. They just wanted to live their lives, and go on these trips without worrying about what the markets are doing on a day-to-day basis.

Current Budget

Compiling a current expense report is one of the trickiest pieces of retirement preparation. Many people assume the expenses of their lives in retirement will be different—lower. After all, there will be no drive to work, no need for a formal wardrobe, and, perhaps most impactful of all, no more saving for retirement!

Yet, we often underestimate our daily spending habits. That's why we typically ask our clients to bring in their bank statements for the past year—they are reflective of your *actual* spending, not just what you think you're spending.

Typically, our clients come in with a retirement income goal in mind. Often, they have a budget they follow based on their current income and lifestyle. Most of our clients enter retirement hoping to avoid a financial step backward like their parents may have done when they retired.

We had one client tell us, "I want to maintain my current lifestyle. When my parents retired, they lived on their fixed incomes in retirement of pensions and Social Security. They stopped living the life they lived when they were in their working years. I want to do more when I retire. I want to travel and do the things I didn't get the chance to do during my working years!"

We hear this quite often. Clients want to maintain their lifestyle, and some even want to spend more when they retire to enjoy all of their hard-working years. They can finally kick back, relax, and enjoy the fruits of their labor.

Everyone's income goal is different, but for most people, they want to maintain the same lifestyle they've grown accustomed to over the years.

To establish your income needs in retirement, we typically suggest starting by figuring out your fixed expenses monthly:
- Rent or mortgage payments
- Car payments
- Other loan payments
- Insurance premiums
- Property taxes
- Phone and utility bills
- Childcare costs
- Tuition fees
- Gym memberships

Now that you have your fixed expenses, start adding your variable expenses together:
- Groceries and dining out
- Clothing
- Personal care
- Entertainment
- Gasoline
- Home and car repairs
- Medical copays

Once you can determine all these expenses with some accuracy, we can then help build an income strategy to cover your expenses in retirement. Obviously, unexpected expenses will come up requiring additional income, such as vacations, etc., but having a solid foundation of retirement income could give you the confidence you need to go an enjoy your hard-earned dollars in your retirement without the concern of running out of money.

We can't count the number of times we've sat with a couple, asked them about their spending, and heard them throw out a number that seemed incredibly low. When we ask them where the number came from, they usually say they estimated based on their total bills. Yet, our spending is so much more than our mortgage, utilities, cable, phone, car, grocery, or credit card bills.

"What about clothes?" we ask, "Or dining out? What about gifts and coffees and last-minute birthday cards?" That's when the lights come on.

This is why we suggest collecting a year's worth of information. There is usually no such thing as a one-time purchase. Did you buy new furniture? Even if that is a rarity, do you think that will be the last time you *ever* buy furniture?

Another hefty expense is spending on the kids. Many of the couples we work with are quick to help their adult children, whether it's something like letting them live in the basement, paying for college, babysitting, paying an occasional bill, or contributing to a grandchild's college fund. Research concluded that 22 percent of adults receive some kind of financial support from parents. That segment jumps to almost 30 percent when factoring the generation we call millennials.[21]

Our clients sometimes protest that what they do for their grown children can stop in retirement. They don't *need* to help. But we get it. Parents like to feel needed. And, while you never want to neglect saving for retirement in favor of taking on financial risks (like your child's student debt), the parents who

---

[21] Kamaron McNair. magnifymoney.com. October 26, 2021. "Nearly 30% of Millenials Still Receive Financial Support From Their Parents."
https://www.magnifymoney.com/blog/news/parental-financial-support-survey

help their adult children do so in part because it helps them feel fulfilled.

When it comes down to expenses, including (and especially) spending on your family, don't make your initial calculations based on what you *could* whittle your budget down to if you *had* to. Instead, start from where you are. Who wants to live off a bare-bones bank account in retirement?

Other Expenses

Once you have nailed down your current budget and your dreams or goals for retirement, there are a few other outstanding pieces to think about—some expenses many people don't take the time to consider before making and executing a plan. But we're assuming you want to get it right, so let's take a look.

Housing

Do you know where you want to live in retirement? This makes up a substantial piece of your income puzzle—since the typical American household owns a home, and it's generally their largest asset.

Some people prefer to live right where they are for as long as they can. Others have been waiting for retirement to pull the trigger on an ambitious move, like purchasing a new house, or even downsizing. Whatever your plans and whatever your reasons, there are quite a few things to consider.

Mortgage
Do you still have a mortgage? What may have been a nice tax boon in your working years could turn into a financial burden in your retirement. After all, when you are on a limited income, a mortgage is just one more bill sapping your financial strength. It is something to put some thought into, whether you plan to age in place or are considering moving to your dream home,

buying a house out of state, or living in a retirement community.

Upkeep and Taxes

A house without a mortgage still requires annual taxes. While it's tempting to think of this as a once-a-year expense, when you have limited earning potential, your annual tax bill might be something into which you should put a little more forethought.

The costs of homeownership aren't just monetary. When you find yourself dealing with more house than you need, it can drain your time and energy. From keeping clutter at bay to keeping the lawn mower running, upkeep can be extensive and expensive. For some, that's a challenge they heartily accept and can comfortably take on. For others, the idea of yard work or cleaning an area larger than they need feels foolish.

For instance, Peggy discovered after her knee replacement that most of her house was inaccessible to her when she was laid up.

"It felt ridiculous to pay someone else to dust and vacuum a house I was only living in 40 percent of!"

Practicality and Adaptability

Erik and Magda are looking to retire within the next two decades. They just sold their old three-bedroom ranch-style house. Their twins are in high school, and the couple has wanted to "upgrade" for years. Now they live in a gorgeous 1940s three-story house with all the kitchen space they ever wanted, five sprawling bedrooms, and a library and media room for themselves and their children. Within months of moving in, the couple realized a house perfect for their active teens would no longer be perfect for them in five to fifteen years.

"We are paying the mortgage for this house, but we've started saving for the next one," said Magda, "because who wants to climb two flights of stairs to their bedroom when they're seventy-eight?"

CAPITALIZE ON RETIREMENT | 47

Others we know have encountered a similar situation in their personal lives. After a health crisis, one couple found the luxurious tub for two they toiled to install had become a specter of a bad slip and a potential safety risk. It's important to think through what your physical reality could be. We always emphasize to our clients that they should plan for whatever their long-term future might hold, but it's amazing how many people don't give it much thought.

Contracts and Regulations

If you are looking into a cross-country move, be aware of new tax tables or local ordinances in the area where you are looking to move. After all, you don't want to experience sticker-shock when you are looking at downsizing or reducing your bills in retirement.

Along the same lines, if you are moving into a retirement community, be sure to look at the fine print. What happens if you must move into a different situation for long-term care? Will you be penalized? Will you be responsible for replacing your slot in the community? What are all the fees, and what do they cover?

Inflation

As we write this in 2022, America has experienced a wave of inflation following a lengthy period of low inflation. Inflation zoomed to 6.8 percent in November 2021, its highest mark since June 1982.[22]

Core inflation is yet another measurement that excludes goods with prices that tend to be more volatile, such as food and energy costs. Core inflation for a 12-month period ending in

---

[22] tradingeconomics.com. 2022 Data/2023 Forecast/1914-2021 Historical. "United States Inflation Rate" https://tradingeconomics.com/united-states/inflation-cpi

May 2022 was 6.2 percent. It so happened energy prices rose a whopping 34.6 percent over that timeframe.[23]

However, inflation isn't a one-time bump; it has a cumulative effect. Again, that can impact the price of groceries greater than other goods. Even with relatively low inflation over the past few decades, an item you bought in 1997 for $2 will cost $3.60 today.[24] Want to go to a show? A $20 ticket in 1997 would cost $40.34 in 2022.[25]

What if, in retirement, we hit a stretch like the late seventies and early eighties, when annual inflation rates of 10 percent became the norm? It may be wise to consider some extra padding in your retirement income plan to account for any potential increase in inflation in the future.

Aging

Also, in the expense category, think about longevity. We all hope to age gracefully. However, it's important to face the prospect of aging with a sense of realism.

The elephant in the room for many families is long-term care: No one wants to admit they will likely need it, but estimates say as many as 70 percent of us will.[26] Aging is a significant piece of retirement income planning because you'll want to figure out how to set aside money for your care, either at home or away from it. The more comfortable you get with discussing your wishes and plans with your loved ones, the easier planning for the financial side of it can be.

---

[23] U.S. Inflation Calculator. "United States Core Inflation Rates (1957-2022)." https://www.usinflationcalculator.com/inflation/united-states-core-inflation-rates
[24] Ibid.
[25] In2013dollars.com "Admission to movies, theaters, and concerts priced at $20 in 1997>$40.34 in 2022" https://www.in2013dollars.com/Admission-to-movies,-theaters,-and-concerts/price-inflation
[26] Moll Law Group. 2022. "The Cost of Long-Term Care." https://www.molllawgroup.com/the-cost-of-long-term-care.html

We discuss health care and potential long-term care costs in more detail elsewhere in this book, but suffice it to say nursing home care tends to be very expensive and typically isn't something you get to choose when you will need.

It isn't just the costs of long-term care that pose a concern in living longer. It's also about covering the possible costs of everything else associated with living longer. For instance, if Henry retires from his job as a biochemical engineer at age sixty-five, perhaps he planned to have a very decent income for twenty years, until age eighty-five. But what if he lives until he's ninety-five? That's a whole third—ten years—more of personal income he will need.

Putting It All Together

Whew! So, you have pulled together what you have, and you have a pretty good idea of where you want to be. Now your financial professional and you can go about the work of arranging what assets you *have* to cover what you *need*—and how you might try to cover any gaps.

Like the proverbial man in the Bible who built his house on a rock, we like to help our clients figure out how to cover their day-to-day living expenses—their needs—with insurance and other guaranteed income sources like pensions and Social Security.

Our Alpha Plan process is built on a four-step process. Our first strategy session is a discovery meeting, where we get to know each other better both personally and professionally.

Once we have all of your financial data, we begin the planning stage, where we analyze your income gap (what you need versus what you have coming in). We then identify strategies and tools to help cover that gap. We calculate the percent return that you need to achieve those goals—if you only need a 2 percent return to be successful in retirement, why shoot for a 25 percent return and risk the potential negative outcome of taking too much risk?

Once we have your income calculated, we show you the recommended structuring of your assets through an investment planning process (allocating into buckets for protection, income, and growth potential).

After investment planning, we move toward tax planning strategies. We calculate and present your tax liability throughout your entire lifetime to find ways we can help minimize that potential burden.

Next, we look at healthcare planning and help you establish your Medicare coverage specific to you and your health situation. We then analyze the long-term care strategies and present what we feel best fits your needs and goals.

Lastly, we discuss legacy planning and any estate planning strategies that can benefit yourself and your heirs.

Each area of planning builds on the other. If we build you a fantastic tax strategy, but you run out of income because investments are not structured appropriately, well, that doesn't work out so well.

Once we get through our first strategy session, we begin to implement the strategies and ensure all the proper tools are in place that help you accomplish your retirement goals.

Once implementation is complete, we begin our monitoring process to assure your plan continues to evolve and operates smoothly as you progress through your golden years.

Again, you should keep in mind there isn't one single financial vehicle, asset, or source to fill all your needs, and that's okay. One of the challenges of planning for your income in retirement concerns figuring out what products and strategies to use. You can release some of that stress when you accept the fact you will probably need a diverse portfolio—potentially with bonds, stocks, insurance, and other income sources—not just one massive money pile.

One way to help shore up your income gaps is by working with your financial professional and a qualified tax advisor to mitigate your tax exposure. If you have a 401(k) or IRA, a tax advisor in your corner can help you figure out how and when to take distributions from your account in a way that doesn't push you into a higher tax bracket. Or you might learn how to use tax-advantaged bonds more effectively. Effective tax planning isn't necessarily about "adding" to your income. Especially regarding retirement, it's less about what you make than it is about what you keep. Paying a lower tax bill keeps more money in your pocket, which is where you want it when it comes to retirement income.

Now you can look at ways to cover your remaining retirement goals. Are there products like long-term care insurance specific to a certain kind of expense you anticipate? Is there a particular asset you want to use for your "play" money—money for trips and gifts for the grandkids? Is there any way you can portion off money for those charitable legacy plans?

Once you have analyzed your income wants, needs, and the assets to realistically cover them, you may have a gap. The masterstroke of a competent financial professional will be to help you figure out how you will cover that gap. Will you need to cut out a round of golf a week? Maybe skip the new car? Or will you need to take more substantial action?

One way to cover an income gap is to consider working longer or even part-time before retirement and even after that magical calendar date. This may not be the best "plan" for you; disabilities, work demands, and physical or emotional limitations can hinder the best-laid plans to continue working. However, if it is physically possible for you, this is one considerable way to help your assets last, for more than one reason.

In fact, 46 percent of the Americans responding to a survey report they plan to work part-time after retiring, while 18 percent indicated they planned to work past the age of seventy.[27]

---

[27] Josephine Nesbit. Go Banking Rates. January 19, 2022. "Nearly Half of Seniors Expect to Work After Retirement — But There Might Be a Better Option." https://www.gobankingrates.com/retirement/planning/nearly-half-of-seniors-expect-to-work-after-retirement-but-there-might-be-a-better-option

When you're retired, you no longer have an employer paying you a steady check. It is up to you to make sure you have saved and planned for the income you need.

CHAPTER 5

Social Security

Social Security is often the foundation of retirement income. Backed by the strength of the U.S. Treasury, it provides perhaps the most dependable paycheck you will have in retirement.

From the time you collect your first paycheck from the job that made you a bona fide taxpayer, you are paying into the grand old Social Security system. What grew and developed out of the pressures of the Great Depression has become one of the most popular government programs in the country, and, if you pay in for the equivalent of ten years or more, you, too, can benefit from the Social Security program.

Now, before we get into the nitty-gritty of Social Security, we'd like to address a current concern: Will Social Security still be there for you when you reach retirement age?

The Future of Social Security

This question is ever-present as headlines trumpet an underfunded Social Security program, alongside the sea of baby boomers who are retiring in droves and the comparatively smaller pool of younger people who are bearing the responsibility of funding the system.

The Social Security Administration itself acknowledges this concern as each Social Security statement now bears an asterisk that continues near the end of the summary:

"*Your estimated benefits are based on current law. Congress has made changes to the law in the past and can do so at any time. The law governing benefit amounts may change because, by 2034, the payroll taxes collected will be enough to pay only about 79 percent of scheduled benefits."

Just a reminder, as if you needed one, that nothing in life is guaranteed. Additionally, depending on who you're listening to, Social Security funds may run low before 2034 thanks to the financial instability and government spending that accompanied the 2020 COVID-19 pandemic.

Before you get too discouraged, though, here are a few thoughts to keep you going:

- Even if the program is only paying 79 cents on the dollar for scheduled benefits, 79 percent is notably not zero.
- The Social Security Administration has made changes in the distant and near past to protect the fund's solvency, including increasing retirement ages and striking certain filing strategies.
- There are many changes Congress could make, and lawmakers are currently discussing how to fix the system, such as further increasing full retirement age and eligibility.
- One thing no one is seriously discussing? Reneging on current obligations to retirees or the soon-to-retire.

Take heart. The real answer to the question, "Will Social Security be there for me?" is still yes.

This question is an important one to consider when you look at how much we, as a nation, rely on this program. Did you know Social Security benefits replace about 40 percent of a person's original income when they retire?[28]

---

[28] ssa.gov. "Alternate Measure of Replacement Rates for Social Security Benefits and Retirement Income"
https://www.ssa.gov/policy/docs/ssb/v68n2/v68n2p1.html

If you ask us, that's a pretty significant piece of your retirement income puzzle.

Another caveat? You may not realize this, but no one can legally "advise" you about your Social Security benefits.

"But, guys," you may be thinking, "isn't that part of what you do? And what about that nice gentleman at the Social Security Administration office I spoke with on the phone?"

Don't get us wrong. Social Security Administration employees know their stuff. They are trained to know policies and programs, and they are usually pretty quick to tell you what you can and cannot do. But the government specifically stipulates, because Social Security is a benefit you alone have paid into and earned, your Social Security decisions, too, are yours alone.

When it comes to financial professionals, we can't push you in any directions, either, *but*—there's a big but here—working with a well-informed financial professional is still incredibly handy when it comes to your Social Security decisions. Why? Because someone who's worth his or her salt will know what withdrawal strategies might pertain to your specific situation and will ask questions that can help you determine what you are looking for when it comes to your Social Security.

For instance, some people want the highest possible monthly benefit. Others want to start their benefits early, not always because of financial need. We heard about one man who called in to start his Social Security payments the day he qualified, just because he liked to think of it as the government paying back a debt it owed him, and he enjoyed the feeling of receiving a check from Uncle Sam.

Whatever your reasons, questions, or feelings regarding Social Security, the decision is yours alone; but working with a financial professional can help you put your options in perspective by showing you—both with industry knowledge and with proprietary software or planning processes—where your benefits fit into your overall strategy for retirement income.

One reason the federal government doesn't allow for "advice" related to Social Security, we suspect, is so no one can profit from giving you advice related to your Social Security benefit—or from providing any clarifications. Again, this is a sign of a good financial professional. Those who are passionate about their work will be knowledgeable about what benefit strategies might be to your advantage and will happily share those possible options with you.

Full Retirement Age

When it comes to Social Security, it seems like many people only think so far as "yes." They don't take the time to understand the various options available. Instead, because it is common knowledge you can begin your benefits at age sixty-two, that's what many of us do. While more people are opting to delay taking benefits, age sixty-two is still firmly the most popular age to start.[29]

What many people fail to understand is, by starting benefits early, they may be leaving a lot of money on the table. You see, the Social Security Administration bases your monthly benefit on two factors: your earnings history and your full retirement age (FRA).

From your earnings history, they pull the thirty-five years you made the most money and use a mathematical indexing formula to figure out a monthly average from those years. If you paid into the system for less than thirty-five years, then every year you didn't pay in will be counted as a zero.

Once they have calculated what your monthly earning would be at FRA, the government then calculates what to put on your check based on how close you are to FRA. FRA was originally set at sixty-five, but, as the population aged and lifespans lengthened, the government shifted FRA later and later, based

---

[29] Chris Kissell. moneytalknews.com. January 20, 2021. "This Is When the Most People Start Taking Social Security."
https://www.moneytalksnews.com/the-most-popular-age-for-claiming-social-security

on an individual's year of birth. Check out the following chart to see when you will reach FRA.[30]

Age to Receive Full Social Security Benefits*	
(Called "full retirement age" [FRA] or "normal retirement age.")	
Year of Birth*	**FRA**
1937 or earlier	65
1938	65 and 2 months
1939	65 and 4 months
1940	65 and 6 months
1941	65 and 8 months
1942	65 and 10 months
1943-1954	66
1955	66 and 2 months
1956	66 and 4 months
1957	66 and 6 months
1958	66 and 8 months
1959	66 and 10 months
1960 and later	67
If you were born on Jan. 1 of any year, you should refer to the previous year. (If you were born on the 1st of the month, we figure your benefit [and your full retirement age] as if your birthday was in the previous month.)	

---

[30] Social Security Administration. "Full Retirement Age." https://www.ssa.gov/planners/retire/retirechart.html

When you reach FRA, you are eligible to receive 100 percent of whatever the Social Security Administration says is your full monthly benefit.

Starting at age sixty-two, for every year before FRA you claim benefits, your monthly check is reduced by 5 percent or more. Conversely, for every year you delay taking benefits past FRA, your monthly benefit increases by 8 percent (until age seventy—after that, there is no monetary advantage to delaying Social Security benefits). While your circumstances and needs may vary, a lot of financial professionals still urge people to at least consider delaying until they reach age seventy.

Why Wait?[31]

| | Taking benefits early could affect your monthly check by _____. |
62	63	64	65	FRA 66	67	68	69	70
-25%	-20%	-13.3%	-6.7%	0	+8%	+16%	+24%	+32%

Social Security

If you are over age thirty, you have probably received a notice from the Social Security Administration telling you to activate something called "My Social Security." This is a handy way to learn more about your particular benefit options, to keep track of what your earnings record looks like, and to calculate the benefits you have accrued over the years.

Essentially, My Social Security is an online account you can activate to see what your personal Social Security picture looks like, which you can do at www.ssa.gov/myaccount. This can be extremely helpful when it comes to planning for income in retirement and figuring up the difference between your anticipated income versus anticipated expenses.

---

[31] Social Security Administration. April 2021. "Can You Take Your Benefits Before Full Retirement Age?"
https://www.ssa.gov/planners/retire/applying2.html

My Social Security is also helpful because it's a great way to see if there is a problem. For instance, we have heard of one woman who, through diligently checking her tax records against her Social Security profile, discovered her Social Security check was shortchanging her, based on her earnings history. After taking the discrepancy to the Social Security Administration, they sent her what they owed her in makeup benefits.

COLA

Social Security is a largely guaranteed piece of the retirement puzzle: If you get a statement that reads you should expect $1,000 a month, you can be sure you will receive $1,000 a month. But there is one variable detail, and that is something called the cost-of-living adjustment, or COLA.

The COLA is an increase in your monthly check meant to address inflation in everyday life. After all, your expenses will likely continue to experience inflation in retirement, but you will no longer have the opportunity for raises, bonuses, or promotions you had when you were working. Instead, Social Security receives an annual cost-of-living increase tied to the Department of Labor's Consumer Price Index for Urban Wage Earners and Clerical Workers, or CPI-W. If the CPI-W measurement shows inflation rose a certain amount for regular goods and services, then Social Security recipients will see that reflected in their COLA.

The COLA averages 4 percent, but in a no- or low-inflation environment, such as in 2010, 2011, and 2016, Social Security recipients will not receive an adjustment. Some view the COLA as a perk, bump, or bonus, but, in reality, it works more like this: Your mom sends you to the store with $2.50 for a gallon of milk. Milk costs exactly $2.50. The next week, you go back with that same amount, but it is now $2.52 for a gallon, so you go back to Mom, and she gives you 2 cents. You aren't bringing home more milk—it just costs more money.

So the COLA is less about "making more money" and more about keeping seniors' purchasing power from eroding when inflation is a big factor, such as in 1975, when it was 8 percent![32] Still, don't let that detract from your enthusiasm about COLAs; after all, what if Mom's solution was: "Here's the same $2.50; try to find pennies from somewhere else to get that milk!"?

Spousal Benefits

We've talked about FRA, but another big Social Security decision involves spousal benefits.

If you or your spouse has a long stretch of zeros in your earnings history—perhaps if one of you stayed home for years, caring for children or sick relatives—you may want to consider filing for spousal benefits instead of filing on your own earnings history. A spousal benefit can be up to 50 percent of the primary wage earner's benefit at full retirement age.

To begin drawing a spousal benefit, you must be at least sixty-two years old, and the primary wage earner must have already filed for his or her benefit. While there are penalties for taking spousal benefits early (you could lose up to 67.5 percent of your check for filing at age sixty-two), you cannot earn credits for delaying past full retirement age.[33]

Like we wrote, the spousal benefit can be a big deal for those who don't have a very long pay history, but it's important to weigh your own earned benefits against the option of withdrawing based on a fraction of your spouse's benefits.

To look at how this could play out, let's use a hypothetical couple: Mary Jane, who is sixty, and Peter, who is sixty-two.

Let's say Peter's benefit at FRA, in his case sixty-six, would be $1,600. If Peter begins his benefits right now, four years before FRA, his monthly check will be $1,200. If Mary Jane

---

[32] Social Security Administration. "Cost-Of-Living Adjustment (COLA) Information for 2022." https://www.ssa.gov/cola

[33] Social Security Administration. "Retirement Planner: Benefits For You As A Spouse." https://www.ssa.gov/planners/retire/applying6.html

begins taking spousal benefits in two years at the earliest date possible, her monthly benefits will be reduced by 67.5 percent, to $520 per month (remember, at FRA, the most she can qualify for is half of Peter's FRA benefit).

What if Peter and Mary Jane both wait until FRA? At sixty-six, Peter begins taking his full benefit of $1,600 a month. Two years later, when she reaches age sixty-six, Mary Jane will qualify for $800 a month. By waiting until FRA, the couple's monthly benefit goes from $1,720 to $2,400.

What if Peter delays until age seventy to get his maximum possible benefit? For each year past FRA he delays, his monthly benefits increase by 8 percent. This means, at seventy, he could file for a monthly benefit of $2,112. However, delayed retirement credits do not affect spousal benefits, so as soon as Peter files at seventy, Mary Jane would also file (at age sixty-eight) for her maximum benefit of $800, so their highest possible combined monthly check is $2,912.[34]

When it comes to your Social Security benefits, you obviously will want to consider whether a monthly check based on a fraction of your spouse's earnings will be comparable to or larger than your own earnings history.

Divorced Spouses

There are a few considerations for those of us who have gone through a divorce. If you 1) were married for ten years or more *and* 2) have since been divorced for at least two years *and* 3) are unmarried *and* 4) your ex-spouse qualifies to begin Social Security, you qualify for a spousal benefit based on your ex-husband or ex-wife's earnings history at FRA. A divorced spousal benefit is different from the married spousal benefit in

---

[34] Office of the Chief Actuary. Social Security Administration. "Social Security Benefits: Benefits for Spouses." https://www.ssa.gov/OACT/quickcalc/spouse.html#calculator

one way: You don't have to wait for your ex-spouse to file before you can file yourself.[35]

For instance, Charles and Moira were married for fifteen years before their divorce, when he was thirty-six and she was forty. Moira has been remarried for twenty years, and, although Charles briefly remarried, his second marriage ended after a few years. Charles' benefits are largely calculated based on his many years of volunteering in schools, meaning his personal monthly benefit is close to zero.

Although Moira has deferred her retirement, opting to delay benefits until she is seventy, Charles can begin taking benefits calculated from Moira's work history at FRA as early as sixty-two. However, he will also have the option of waiting until FRA to collect the maximum, or 50 percent of Moira's earned monthly benefit at her FRA.

Widowed Spouses

If your marriage ended with the death of your spouse, you might claim a benefit for your spouse's earned income as his or her widow/widower, called a survivor's benefit. Unlike a spousal benefit or divorced benefits, if your husband or wife dies, you can claim his or her full benefit. Also, unlike spousal benefits, if you need to, you can begin taking income when you turn sixty. However, as with other benefit options, your monthly check will be permanently reduced for withdrawing benefits before FRA.

If your spouse began taking benefits before he or she died, you can't delay withdrawing your survivor's benefits to get delayed credits. The Social Security Administration maintains

---

[35] Social Security Administration. "Retirement Planner: If You Are Divorced." https://www.ssa.gov/planners/retire/divspouse.html

you can only get as much from a survivor's benefit as your deceased spouse might have received, had he or she lived.[36]

Taxes, Taxes, Taxes

With Social Security, as with everything, it is important to consider taxes. It may be surprising, but your Social Security benefits are not tax-free. Despite having been taxed to accrue those benefits in the first place, you may have to pay Uncle Sam income taxes on up to 85 percent of your Social Security.

The Social Security Administration figures these taxes using what they call "the provisional income formula." Your provisional income formula differs from the adjusted gross income you use for your regular income taxes. Instead, to find out how much of your Social Security benefit is taxable, the Social Security Administration calculates it this way:

Provisional Income = Adjusted Gross Income + Nontaxable Interest + ½ of Social Security

See that piece about nontaxable interest? That generally means interest from government bonds and notes. It surprises many people that, although you may not pay taxes on those assets, their income will count against you when it comes to Social Security taxation.

Once you have figured out your provisional income (also called "combined income"), you can use the following chart to figure out your Social Security taxes.[37]

---

[36] Social Security Administration. "Social Security Benefit Amounts For The Surviving Spouse By Year Of Birth." https://www.ssa.gov/planners/survivors/survivorchartred.html

[37] Social Security Administration. "Benefits Planner: Income Taxes and Your Social Security Benefits." https://www.ssa.gov/planners/taxes.html

Taxes on Social Security

Provisional Income = Adjusted Gross Income + Nontaxable Interest + ½ of Social Security

If you are ___ and your provisional income is ___, then...		Uncle Sam will tax ___ of your Social Security
Single	Married, filing jointly	
Less than $25,000	Less than $32,000	0%
$25,000 to $34,000	$32,000 to $44,000	Up to 50%
More than $34,000	More than $44,000	Up to 85%

This is one more reason it may benefit you to work with financial and tax professionals: They can look at your entire financial picture to make your overall retirement plan as tax-efficient as possible—including your Social Security benefit.

Working and Social Security: The Earnings Test

If you haven't reached FRA, but you started your Social Security benefits and are still working, things get a little hairy.

Because you have started Social Security payments, the Social Security Administration will pay out your benefits (at that reduced rate, of course, because you haven't reached your FRA). Yet, because you are working, the organization must also withhold from your check to add to your benefits, which you are already collecting. See how this complicates matters?

To address the situation, the government has what is called the earnings test. For 2022, you can earn up to $19,560 without it affecting your Social Security check. But, for every $2 you

CAPITALIZE ON RETIREMENT | 65

earn past that amount, the Social Security Administration will withhold $1. The earnings test loosens in the year of your FRA; if you are reaching FRA in 2022, you can earn up to $51,960 before you run into the earnings test, and the government only withholds $1 for every $3 past that amount. The month you reach FRA, you are no longer subject to any earnings withholding. For instance, if you are still working and will turn sixty-six on December 28, 2022, you would only have to worry about the earnings test until December, and then you can ignore it entirely. Keep in mind, the money the government withholds from your Social Security benefits while you are working before FRA will be tacked back onto your benefits check after FRA.[38]

This is why it's so important to know your income goal up front. This way, we can determine exactly what mix of Social Security and investments it will take to help get you there. The income you received from your paychecks during your working years will need to be replaced, and, in some cases, Social Security payouts can be a big help in that regard. Still, it's highly likely you'll need income from other sources as well.

Knowing when to begin receiving Social Security payouts makes a big difference in how much income you'll receive, how often, and for how long. We'll take a look at where you are now financially and where you hope to be ten or twenty years down the road. We then devise a strategy designed to help you to take Social Security in the most efficient manner for your unique situation.

---

[38] Social Security Administration. "Exempt Amounts Under the Earnings Test." https://www.ssa.gov/oact/cola/rtea.html

CHAPTER 6

401(k)s & IRAs

Have you heard? Today's retirement is not your parents' retirement. You see, back in the day, it was pretty common to work for one company for the vast majority of your career and then retire with a gold watch and a pension.

The gold watch was a symbol of the quality time you had put in at that company, but the pension was more than a symbol. Instead, it was a guarantee—as solid as your employer—that they would repay your hard work with a certain amount of income in your old age. Did you see the caveat there? Your pension's guarantee was *as solid as your employer*. The problem was, what if your employer went under?

Companies that failed couldn't pay their retired employees' pensions, leading to financial challenges for many. Beginning in 1974 with Congress' passage of the Employee Retirement Income Security Act, federal legislation and regulations aimed at protecting retirees were everywhere. One piece of legislation included a relatively obscure section of the Internal Revenue Code, added in 1978. Section 401(k), to be specific.

IRC section 401, subsection k, created tax advantages for employer-sponsored financial products, even if the main contributor was the employee him or herself. Over the years, more employers took note, beginning an age of transition away from pensions and toward 401(k) plans. A 401(k) is a retirement account with certain tax benefits and restrictions on the investments or other financial products inside of it.

Essentially, 401(k)s and their individual retirement account (IRA) counterparts are "wrappers" that provide tax benefits around assets; typically, the assets that compose IRAs and 401(k)s are mutual funds, stock and bond mixes, and money market accounts. However, IRA and 401(k) contents are becoming more diverse these days, with some companies offering different kinds of annuity options within their plans.

Where pensions are defined-*benefit* plans, 401(k)s and IRAs are defined-*contribution* plans. The one-word change outlines the basic difference. Pensions spell out what you can expect to receive from the plan but not necessarily how much money it will take to fund those benefits. With 401(k)s, an employer sets a standard for how much they will contribute (if any), and you can be certain of what you are contributing. Still, there is no outline for what you can expect to receive in return for those contributions.

Modern employment looks very different. A 2018 survey by the Bureau of Labor Statistics determined U.S. workers stayed with their employers a median of about four years. Workers ages fifty-five to sixty-four had a little more staying power and were most likely to stay with their employer for about ten years.[39] Participation in 401(k) plans has steadily risen this century, totaling $7.3 trillion in assets in 2021 compared to $3.1 trillion in 2011. About 60 million active participants engaged in 401(k) plans in 2020.[40]

A far cry from a pension and gold watch, wouldn't you say?

If there is anything to learn from this paradigm shift, it's that you must look out for yourself. Whether you have worked for a company for two years or twenty, you are still the one who has to look out for your own best interests. That holds doubly true

---

[39] Bureau of Labor Statistics. September 22, 2020. "Employee Tenure Summary." https://www.bls.gov/news.release/tenure.nr0.htm
[40] Investment Company Institute. October 11, 2021. "Frequently Asked Questions About 401(k) Plan Research."
https://www.ici.org/faqs/faq/401k/faqs_401k

when it comes to preparing for retirement. If you are one of the lucky ones who still has a pension, good for you. But for the rest of us, it is likely a 401(k)—or possibly one of its nonprofit- or government-sector counterparts, a 403(b) or 457 plan—is one of your biggest assets for retirement.

No matter what form of workplace benefit you're partaking in, it's important to keep tabs on its tax ramifications. We have one client, who we'll call Bill, who was one of the lucky few to continue receiving a pension from his employer. He was set to receive $7,000 a month, and that's not including his Social Security.

Like the story we told earlier about Charlie and Betty, he would have more retirement income than he needed. On the surface, the idea of receiving thousands per month for the hard work you put into your career sounds like a good thing. However, he would also be pushed into a higher tax bracket. With RMDs factored in, that shift could have become a major problem.

Many people who meet with us aren't aware they've got a silent partner—the U.S. government—that will be taking its share of these retirement distributions through taxes. When we first meet with people and share this knowledge, it's a good feeling to know you may be able to help prevent them from potentially paying thousands of extra dollars in taxes down the road. Without all the information, you can't make the best decision.

As pensions fall by the wayside, some employers offer incentives to contribute to their company plans, like a company match. On that subject, we have one thing to say: *Do it!* Nothing in life is free, as they say, but a company match on your retirement funds is about as close to free money as it gets. If you can make the minimum to qualify for your company's match at all, go for it.

Now, it's likely, during our working years, we mostly "set and forget" our 401(k) funding. Because it is tax-advantaged, your employer is taking money from your paycheck—before taxes—and putting it into your plan for you. Maybe you got to pick a selection of investments, or maybe your company only offers one choice of investment in your 401(k). Either way, while you are gainfully employed, your most impactful decision may just be the decision to continue funding your plan in the first place. But, when you are ready to retire or move jobs, you have choices to make requiring a little more thought and care.

When you are ready to part ways with your job, you have a few options:

- Leave the money where it is
- Take the cash (and pay income taxes and perhaps a 10 percent additional federal tax if you are younger than age fifty-nine-and-one-half)
- Transfer the money to another employer plan (if the new plan allows)
- Roll the money over into a self-directed IRA

Now, these are just general options. You will have to decide, hopefully with the help of a financial professional, what's right for you. For instance, 401(k)s are typically pretty closely tied to the companies offering them, so when changing jobs, it may not always be possible to transfer a 401(k) to another 401(k). Leaving the money where it is may also be out of the question—some companies have direct cash payout or rollover policies once someone is no longer employed.

Also, remember what we mentioned earlier about how we change jobs more often these days? That means you likely have a 401(k) with your current company, but you may also have a string of retirement accounts trailing you from other jobs.

When it comes to your retirement income, it's important to be able to pull together *all* your assets, so you can examine what you have and where, and then decide what you will do with it.

Tax-Qualified, Tax-Preferred, Tax-Deferred ... Still TAXED

Financial media often cite IRAs and 401(k)s for their tax benefits. After all, with traditional plans, you put your money in, pre-tax, and it hopefully grows for years, even decades, untaxed. That's why these accounts are called "tax-qualified" or "tax-deferred" assets. They aren't *tax-free!* Rarely does Uncle Sam allow business to continue without receiving his piece of the pie, and your retirement assets are no different. If you didn't pay taxes on the front end, you will pay taxes on the money you withdraw from these accounts in retirement. Don't get us wrong: This isn't an inherently good or bad thing; it's just the way it is. It's important to understand, though, for the sake of planning ahead.

In retirement, many people assume they will be in a lower tax bracket. Are you planning to pare down your lifestyle in retirement? Perhaps you are, and perhaps you will have substantially less income in retirement. But many of our clients tell us they want to live life more or less the same as they always have. The money they would previously have spent on business attire or gas for their commute they now want to spend on hobbies and grandchildren. That's all fine, and for many of them, it is doable, but does it put them in a lower tax bracket? Probably not.

Keep in mind, IRAs, 401(k)s, and their alternatives have a few limitations because of their special tax status. For one thing, the IRS sets limits on your contributions to these retirement accounts. If you are contributing to a 401(k) or an equivalent nonprofit or government plan, your annual contribution limit is $20,500 (as of 2022). If you are fifty or older, the IRS allows additional contributions, called "catch-up contributions," of up to $6,500 on top of the regular limit of

$20,500.[41] For an IRA, the limit is $7,000, with a catch-up limit of an additional $1,000.[42]

Because their tax advantages come from their intended use as retirement income, withdrawing funds from these accounts before you turn fifty-nine-and-one-half can carry stiff penalties. In addition to fees your investment management company might charge, you will have to pay income tax *and* a 10 percent federal tax penalty, with few exceptions.

The fifty-nine-and-one-half rule for retirement accounts is incredibly important to remember, especially when you're young. Younger workers are often tempted to cash out an IRA from a previous employer and then are surprised to find their checks missing 20 percent of the account value to income taxes, penalty taxes, and account fees.

Many millennials we see in our practice say, while they may be socking money away in their workplace retirement plan, it is often the *only* place they are saving. This could be problematic later because of the fifty-nine-and-one-half rule; what if you have an emergency? It is important to fund your retirement, but you need to have some liquid assets handy as emergency funds. This can help you avoid breaking into your retirement accounts and incurring taxes and penalties because of the fifty-nine-and-one-half rule.

RMDs

Remember how we talked about the 401(k) or IRA being a "tax wrapper" for your funds? Well, eventually, Uncle Sam will want a bite of that candy bar. So, when you turn seventy-two, the government requires you withdraw a portion of your account, which the IRS calculates based on the size of your account and

---

[41] Jackie Stewart. Kiplinger.com. Dec. 17, 2021. "401(k) Contribution Limits for 2022" https://www.kiplinger.com/retirement/retirement-plans/401ks/603949/401k-contribution-limits-for-2022
[42] Fidelity.com. 2021."IRA contribution limits."
https://www.fidelity.com/retirement-ira/contribution-limits-deadlines

your estimated lifespan. This required minimum distribution, or RMD, is the government's insurance it will collect some taxes, at some point, from your earnings. Because you didn't pay taxes on the front end, you will now pay income taxes on whatever you withdraw, including your RMDs. Also, let us just remind you not to play chicken with the U.S. government; if you don't take your RMDs starting at seventy-two, you will have to write a check to the IRS for *50 percent* of the amount of your missed RMDs. With the change in law from the SECURE Act of 2019, even after you begin RMDs, you can still also continue contributing to your 401(k) or IRAs if you are still employed, which can affect the whole discussion on RMDs and possible tax considerations.

If you don't need income from your retirement accounts, RMDs can seem like more of a tax burden than an income boon. While some people prefer to reinvest their RMDs, this comes with the possibility of additional taxation: You'll pay income taxes on your RMDs and then capital gains taxes on the growth of your investments. If you are legacy minded, there are other ways to use RMDs, many of which have tax benefits.

Permanent Life Insurance
One way to turn those pesky RMDs into a legacy is through permanent life insurance. Assuming you need the death benefit coverage and can qualify for it medically, if properly structured, these products can pass on a sizeable death benefit to your beneficiaries, tax-free, as part of your general legacy plan.

ILIT
Another way to use RMDs toward your legacy is to work with an estate planning attorney to create an irrevocable life insurance trust (ILIT). This is basically a permanent life insurance policy placed within a trust. Because the trust is irrevocable, you would relinquish control of it, but, unlike with just a permanent life insurance policy, your death benefit won't count toward your taxable estate.

Annuities

Because annuities can be tax-deferred, using all or a portion of your RMDs to fund an annuity contract can be one way to further delay taxation while guaranteeing your income payments (either to you or your loved ones) later. (Assuming you don't need the RMD income during your retirement.)

Qualified Charitable Distributions

If you are charity-minded, you may use your RMDs toward a charitable organization instead of using them for income. You must do this directly from your retirement account (you can't take the RMD check and *then* pay the charity) for your withdrawals to be qualified charitable distributions (QCDs), but this is one way of realizing some of the benefits of a charitable legacy during your own lifetime. You will not need to pay taxes on your QCDs, and they won't count toward your annual charitable tax deduction limit, plus you'll be able to see how the organization you are supporting uses your donations. You should consult a financial professional on how to correctly make a QCD, particularly since the SECURE Act has implemented a few regulations on this point.[43]

Roth IRA

Since the Taxpayer Relief Act of 1997, there has been a different kind of retirement account, or "tax wrapper," available to the public: the Roth. Roth IRAs and Roth 401(k)s each differ from their traditional counterparts in one big way: You pay your taxes on the front end. This means, once your post-tax money is in the Roth IRA or Roth 401(k), as long as you follow the rules and limitations of that account, your distributions are truly tax-free. You won't pay income tax when you take withdrawals, so,

---

[43] Bob Carlson. Forbes. January 28, 2020. "More Questions And Answers About The SECURE Act."
https://www.forbes.com/sites/bobcarlson/2020/01/28/more-questions-and-answers-about-the-secure-act/#113d49564869

in turn, you don't have to worry about RMDs. However, Roth accounts have the same limitations as traditional 401(k)s and IRAs when it comes to withdrawing money before age fifty-nine-and-one-half, with the added stipulation that the account must have been open for at least five years in order for the accountholder to make withdrawals.

It's very common for our clients to do Roth conversions. How that conversion is executed is very specific based on each person's unique situation. When done correctly, a conversion can help someone who is in, say, the 22 percent tax bracket stay there, rather than taking RMDs or another form of excess income that would have pushed them up into the 25 percent tax bracket, if not higher.

Taking Charge

As mentioned earlier, the 401(k) and IRA have largely replaced pensions, but they aren't an equal trade.

Pensions are employer-funded; the money feeding into them is money that wouldn't ever show up on your pay stub. Because 401(k)s are self-funded, you must actively and consciously save. This distinction has made a difference when it comes to funding retirement. The average 401(k) balance for a person age sixty to sixty-nine is $198,600, but the median likely tells the full story. The median 401(k) balance for a person age sixty to sixty-nine is $62,000. A general suggestion derived from those statistics is to aim, by age thirty, to have saved an amount equal to 50 to 100 percent of your annual salary.[44] For some thirty-year-olds, saving half an annual salary by age thirty is more than some sixty-to-sixty-nine-year-olds have saved for their entire lives

There can be many reasons why people underfund their retirement plans, like being overwhelmed by the investment

---

[44] Arielle O'Shea. Nerd Wallet. March 17, 2021. "The Average 401(k) Balance by Age." https://www.nerdwallet.com/article/investing/the-average-401k-balance-by-age

choices or taking withdrawals from IRAs when they leave an employer, but the reason at the top of the list is this: People simply aren't participating to begin with.

So, whether you use a 401(k) with an employer or an IRA alternative with a private company, separate from your workplace, the most important retirement savings decision you can make is to sock away your money somewhere in the first place.

CHAPTER 7

Annuities

In our practice, we offer our clients a variety of products—from securities to insurance—all designed to help them reach their financial goals. You may be wondering: Why single out a single product in this book?

Well, while most of our clients have a pretty good understanding of business and finance, we sometimes find those who have the impression there must be magic involved. Some people assume there is a magic finance wand we can wave to change years' worth of savings into a strategy for retirement income. But it's not as easy as a goose laying golden eggs or the Fairy Godmother turning a pumpkin into a coach!

Finances aren't magic; it takes lots of hard work and, typically, several financial products and strategies to pull together a complete retirement plan. Of all the financial products we work with, it seems people find none more mysterious than annuities. And, if we may say, even some of those who recognize the word "annuity" have a limited understanding of the product. So, in the interest of demystifying annuities, let us tell you a little about what an annuity is.

In general, insurance is a financial hedge against risk. Car owners buy auto insurance to protect their finances in case they injure someone or someone injures them. Homeowners have house insurance to protect their finances in case of a fire, flood, or another disaster. People have life insurance to protect their finances in case of untimely death. Almost juxtaposed to life insurance, people have annuities in case of a long life; annuities can give you financial protection by providing consistent and reliable income payments.

The basic premise of an annuity is you, the annuitant, pay an insurance company some amount in exchange for their contractual guarantee they will pay you income for a certain time period. How that company pays you, for how long, and how much they offer are all determined by the annuity contract you enter into with the insurance company.

How You Get Paid

There are two ways for an annuity contract to provide income: The first is through what is called annuitization, and the second is through the use of income riders. We'll get into income riders in a bit, but let's talk about annuitization. That nice, long word is, in our opinion, one reason annuities have a reputation for mystery and misinformation.

Annuitization

When someone "annuitizes" a contract, it is the point where he or she turns on the income stream. Once a contract has been annuitized, there is no going back. With annuities, if the policyholder lives longer than the insurance company planned, the insurance company is still obligated to pay him or her, even if the payments end up being way more than the contract's actual value. If, however, the policyholder dies an untimely death, depending on the contract type, the insurance company may keep anything left of the money that funded the annuity—nothing would be paid out to the contract holder's survivors. You see where that could make some people balk? Now, modern annuities rarely rely on annuitization for the income portion of the contract, and instead have so many bells and whistles that the old concept of annuitization seems outdated, but because this is still an option, it's important to at least understand the basic concept.

Riders

Speaking of bells and whistles, let's talk about riders. Modern annuities have a lot of different options these days, many in the form of riders you can add to your contract for a fee—usually about 1 percent of the contract value per year. Each rider has its particulars, and the types of riders available will vary by the type of annuity contract purchased, but we'll just briefly outline some of these little extras:

- Lifetime income rider: Contract guarantees you an enhanced income for life
- Death benefit rider: Contract pays an enhanced death benefit to your beneficiaries even if you have annuitized
- Return of premium rider: Guarantees you (or your beneficiaries) will at least receive back the premium value of the annuity
- Long-term care rider: Provides a certain amount, sometimes as much as twice the principal value of the contract, to help pay for long-term care if the contract holder is moved to a nursing home or assisted living situation

This isn't an extensive look, and usually the riders have fancier names based on the issuing company, like "Lorem Ipsum Insurance Company Income Preferred Bonus Fixed Index Annuity rider," but we just wanted to show you what some of the general options are in layperson's terms.

Types of Annuities

Annuities break down into four basic types: immediate, variable, fixed, and fixed index.

Immediate

Immediate annuities primarily rely on annuitization to provide income—you give the insurance company a lump sum up front, and your payments begin immediately. Once you begin receiving income payments, the transaction is irreversible, and you no longer have access to your money in a lump sum. When you die, any remaining contract value is typically forfeited to the insurance company.

All other annuity contract types are "deferred" contracts, meaning you fund your policy as a lump sum or over a period of years and you give it the opportunity to grow over time—sometimes years, sometimes decades.

Variable

A variable annuity is an insurance contract as well as an investment. It's sold by insurance companies, but only through someone who is registered to sell investment products. With a variable annuity contract, the insurance company invests your premiums in subaccounts that are tied to the stock market. This makes it a bit different from the other annuity contract types because it is the only contract where your money is subject to losses because of market declines. Your contract value has a greater opportunity to grow, but it also stands to lose. Additionally, your contract's value will be subject to the underlying investment's fees and limitations—including capital gains taxes, management fees, etc. Once it is time for you to receive income from the contract, the insurance company will pay you a certain income, locked in at whatever your contract's value was.

Fixed

A traditional fixed annuity is pretty straightforward. You purchase a contract with a guaranteed interest rate and, when you are ready, the insurance company will make regular income payments to you at whatever payout rate your contract guarantees. Those payments will continue for the rest of your life and, if you choose, for the remainder of your spouse's life.

Fixed annuities don't have much in the way of upside potential, but many people like them for their guarantees (after all, if your Aunt May lives to be ninety-five, knowing she has a paycheck later in life can be her mental and financial safety net), as well as for their predictability. Unlike variable annuities, which are subject to market risk and might be up one year and down the next, you can easily calculate the value of your fixed annuity over your lifetime.

Fixed Index

To recap, variable annuities take on more risk to offer more possibilities to grow. Fixed annuities have less potential growth, but they protect your principal. In the last couple of decades, many insurance companies have retooled their product line to offer fixed index annuities, which are sort of midway between variable and fixed annuities on that risk/reward spectrum. Fixed index annuities offer greater growth potential than traditional fixed annuities but less than variable annuities. Like traditional fixed annuities, however, fixed index annuities are protected from downside market losses.

Fixed index annuities earn interest that is tied to the market, meaning that, instead of your contract value growing at a set interest rate like a traditional fixed annuity, it has the potential to grow within a range. Your contract's value is credited interest based on the performance of an external market index like the S&P 500 while never being invested in the market itself. You can't invest in the S&P 500 directly, but each year, your annuity as the potential to earn interest based on the chosen index's performance, submit to limits set by the company such as caps, spreads and participation rates. For instance, if your contract caps your interest at 5 percent, then in a year that the S&P 500 gains 3 percent, your annuity value increases 3 percent. If the S&P 500 gains 35 percent, your annuity value gets a 5 percent interest bump. But since your money isn't actually invested in the market with a fixed index annuity, if the market nosedives (such as happened during 2000, 2008 and 2020, anyone?) you won't see any increase in your contract value. Conversely, there will also be no decrease in your contract value—no matter how badly the market performed, as long as you follow the terms of the contract, you won't lose any of the interest you were credited in previous years.

So, what if the S&P 500 shows a market loss of 30 percent? Your contract value isn't going anywhere (unless you purchased an optional rider—this charge will still come out of your annuity value each year). For those who are more interested in protection than growth potential, fixed index annuities can be an attractive option because, when the stock market has a long period of positive performance, a fixed index annuity can enjoy conservative growth. And, during stretches where the stock market is erratic and stock values across the board take significant losses? Fixed index annuities won't lose anything due to the stock market volatility.

When asked their stance on fixed index annuities, many advisors may run from the question. We believe there is a stereotype about these products, and a lot of people have strong opinions on the effectiveness of FIAs. Personally, we recommend them often, where appropriate. Our main focus aligns with that of many retirees': getting competitive growth potential with less risk of losing hard-earned money.

FIAs can help address some of those needs. The FIA can earn interest periodically if the selected market index has risen, and cannot decrease due to market loss. The guaranteed income stream also means reliability, which may be the most important factor for a retiree who is no longer receiving regular paychecks from a job.

Other Things to Know About Annuities

We just talked about the four kinds of annuity contracts available, but all of them have some commonalities as annuities.

For all annuities, the contractual guarantees are only as strong as the insurance company that sells the product, which makes it important to thoroughly check the credit ratings of any company whose products you are considering.

Annuities are tax-deferred, meaning you don't have to pay taxes on interest earnings each year as the contract value grows. Instead, you will pay ordinary income taxes on your withdrawals. These are meant to be long-term products, so, like other tax-deferred or tax-advantaged products, if you begin taking withdrawals from your contract before age fifty-nine-and-one-half, you may also have to pay a 10 percent federal tax penalty. Also, while annuities are generally considered illiquid, most contracts allow you to withdraw up to 10 percent of your contract value every year. Withdraw any more, however, and you could incur additional surrender penalties.

Keep in mind, your withdrawals will deplete the accumulated cash value, death benefit, and, possibly, the rider values of your contract.

We find the opinion on annuities has changed since the 1980s, and for good reason. Not too long ago, "annuity" was often seen as a dirty word, but that may be a result of misconceptions about what these vehicles can do. We often use annuities to help fill an income gap people encounter in retirement, and sometimes find them to be a good alternative to bonds, which were a more profitable investment in decades past.

Annuities aren't for everyone, but it's important to understand them before saying "yea" or "nay" on whether they fit into your plan; otherwise, you're not operating with complete information, wouldn't you agree? Regardless, you should talk to a financial professional who can help you understand annuities, help you dissect your particular financial needs, and help show you whether an annuity is appropriate for your retirement income plan.

Annuity guarantees rely on the financial strength and claims-paying ability of the issuing insurance company. Annuities are insurance products that may be subject to fees, surrender charges, and holding periods, which vary by state. Annuities are not FDIC insured.

CHAPTER 8

Estate & Legacy

In our practice, we devote a significant portion of our time to matters of estates. That doesn't mean drawing up wills or trusts or putting together powers of attorney or anything like that. After all, we're not an estate planning attorney. But we are financial professionals, and what part of the "estate" isn't affected by money matters?

We've included this chapter because we have seen many people do estate planning wrong. Clients, or clients' families, have come in after experiencing a death in the family and have found themselves in the middle of probate, high taxes, or a discovery of something unforeseen (often long-term care) draining the estate.

We have also seen people do estate planning right: clients or families who visit our office to talk about legacies and how to make them last and adult children who have room to grieve without an added burden of unintended costs, without stress from a family ruptured because of inadequate planning.

We'll share some of these stories here. However, we're not going to give you specific advice, since everyone's situation is unique. We only want to give you some things to think about and to underscore the importance of planning ahead.

We have a strategic partnership with an attorney, which allows us to refer clients to someone we know and trust to handle any legal issues that may arise leading up to and during retirement.

You Can't Take It With You

When it comes to legacy and estate planning, the most important thing is to *do it*. We have heard people from clients to celebrities (rap artist Snoop Dogg comes to mind) say they aren't interested in what happens to their assets when they die because they'll be dead. That's certainly one way to look at it. But we think that's a very selfish way to go about things—we all have people and causes we care about, and those who care about us. Even if the people we love don't *need* what we leave behind, they can still be fined or legally tied up in the probate process or burial costs if we don't plan for those. And that's not even considering what happens if you become incapacitated at some point while you are still alive. Having a plan in place can greatly reduce the stress of those responsibilities on your loved ones; it's just a loving thing to do.

Documents

There are a few documents that lay the groundwork of legacy planning. You've probably heard of all or most of them, but we'd like to review what they are and how people commonly use them. These are all things you should talk about with an estate planning attorney to establish your legacy.

Powers of Attorney

A power of attorney, or POA, is a document giving someone the authority to act on your behalf and in your best interests. These come in handy in situations where you cannot be present (think a vacation where you get stuck in Canada) or, for durable powers of attorney, even when you are incapacitated (think in a coma or coping with dementia).

It is important to have powers of attorney in place and to appoint someone you trust to act on your behalf in these matters. Have you ever heard of someone who was incapacitated after a car accident, whether from head trauma or being in a coma for weeks—sometimes months? Do you think their bills stopped coming due during that time? We like our phone company and our bank, but neither one is about to put a moratorium on sending us bills, particularly not for an extended or interminable period. A power of attorney would have the authority to pay your mortgage or cancel your cable while you are unable.

You can have multiple POAs and require them to act jointly.
What this looks like: Do you think two heads are better than one? One man, Chris, significantly relied on his two sons' opinions for both his business and personal matters. He appointed both sons as joint POA, requiring both their signoffs for his medical and financial matters.

You can have multiple POAs who can act independently.
What this looks like: Irene had three children with whom she routinely stayed. They lived in different areas of the country, which she thought was an advantage; one month she might be hiking out West, the next she could enjoy the newest off-Broadway production, and the next she could soak up some Southern sun. She named her three children as independently authorized POAs, so, if something happened, no matter where she was, the child closest could step in to act on her behalf.

You can have POAs who have different responsibilities.
What this looks like: Although Luke's friend Claire, a nurse, was his go-to and POA for health-related issues, financial matters usually made her nervous, so he appointed his good neighbor, Matt, as his POA in all of his financial and legal matters.

In addition to POAs, it may be helpful to have an advanced medical directive. This is a document where you have pre-decided what choices you would make about different health scenarios. An advanced medical directive can help ease the burden for your medical POA and loved ones, particularly when it comes to end-of-life care.

Wills

Perhaps the most basic document of legacy planning, a will is a legal document wherein you outline your wishes for your estate. When it comes to your estate after your death, having a will is the foundation of your legacy. Without one, your loved ones are left behind, guessing what you would have wanted, and the court will likely split your assets according to the state's defaults. Maybe that's exactly what you wanted, as far as anyone knows, right? Because even if you told your nephew he could have your car he's been driving, if it's not in writing, it still might go to the brother, sister, son, or daughter to whom you aren't speaking.

However, it may not be enough just to have a will. Even with a will, your assets will be subject to probate. Probate is what we call the state's process for determining a will's validity. A judge will go through your will to question if it conflicts with state law, if it is the most up-to-date document, if you were mentally competent at the time it was in order, etc. For some, this is a quick, easily-resolved process. For others, particularly if someone steps forward to contest the will, it may take years to settle, all the while subjecting the assets to court costs and attorney's fees.

One other undesirable piece of the probate process is that it is a public process. That means anyone can go to the courthouse, ask for copies of the case, and discover your assets. They can also see who is slated to receive what and who is disputing.

We have heard stories of people losing as much as 5 to 10 percent of their entire estate to probate cases. Nobody wins in these situations, as every cent of that money could have instead gone to the deceased's loved ones. For that reason, we always make it a priority to clearly establish our clients' beneficiaries.

It's also important to remember beneficiary lines trump wills. So, that large life insurance policy? What if, when you bought it fifteen years ago, you wrote your ex-husband's name on the beneficiary line? Even if you stipulate otherwise in your will, the company that holds your policy will pay out to your ex-spouse. Or, how about the thousands of dollars in your IRA you dedicated to the children thirty years ago, but one of your children was killed in a car accident, leaving his wife and two toddlers behind? That IRA is going to transfer to your remaining children, with nothing for your daughter-in-law and grandchildren.

That may paint a grim portrait, but we can't underscore enough the importance of working with a skilled estate planning attorney to keep your will and beneficiary lines up to date as your life changes, for the sake of your loved ones.

One client family we work with has a son with special needs. When they first came to us, their estate plan was set up so their assets would flow directly to their child. That may sound logical enough, yet in this specific case, it could have led to major problems down the road.

The reason that's so important is because he is basically receiving disability benefits, a need that will continue after his parents pass. If his parents' assets flowed into his name instead of a trust, he would lose those benefits.

This scenario serves as just one example of the type of details we look for when helping our clients with their unique estate planning needs. For this family, the question was, "How can we make these assets flow the right way, so that the clients' son is not negatively affected and still taken care of?" There are a lot of technicalities to consider, and if we didn't partner with an attorney to offer thistype of planning and set up a trust, it's possible the parents' assets would have been held from their son, leaving him with a major inconvenience after they passed away.

Trusts

Another piece of legacy planning to consider is the trust.

A trust is set up through an attorney and allows a third party, or trustee, to hold your assets and determine how they will pass to your beneficiaries. Many people are skeptical of trusts because they assume trusts are only appropriate for the fabulously wealthy.

However, a simple trust will likely cost more than $1,000 if prepared by an attorney and fees can be higher for couples.[45] But a trust can help you avoid both the expense and publicity of probate, provide a more immediate transfer of wealth, avoid some taxes, and provide you greater control over your legacy.

For instance, if you want to set aside some funds for a grandchild's college education, you can make it a requirement he or she enrolls in classes before your trust will dispense any funds. Like a will, beneficiary lines will override your trust conditions, so you must still keep insurance policies and other assets up to date.

Like any financial or legal consideration, there are many options these days beyond the simple "yes or no" question of whether to have a trust. For one thing, you will need to consider if you want your trust to be revocable (you can change the terms while you are alive) or irrevocable (can't be changed; you are no longer the "owner" of the contents). A brief note here about irrevocable trusts: Although they have significant and greater tax benefits, they are still subject to a Medicaid look-back period. This means, if you transfer your assets into an irrevocable trust in an attempt to shelter them from a Medicaid spend-down, you will be ineligible for Medicaid coverage of

---

[45] Rickie Houston. smartasset.com. "How Much Does It Cost to Set Up a Trust? https://smartasset.com/estate-planning/how-much-does-it-cost-to-set-up-a-trust

long-term care for five years. Yet, an irrevocable trust can avoid both probate and estate taxes, and it can even protect assets from legal judgments against you.

Another thing to remember when it comes to trusts, in general, is, even if you have set up a trust, you must remember to fund it. In our years work, we've had numerous clients come to us, assuming they have protected their assets with a trust. When we talk about taxes and other pieces of their legacy, it turns out they never retitled any assets or changed any paperwork on the assets they wanted in the trust. So, please remember, a trust is just a bunch of fancy legal papers if you haven't followed through on retitling your assets.

Taxes

Although charitable contributions, trusts, and other tax-efficient strategies can reduce your tax bill, it's unlikely your estate will be passed on entirely tax-free. Yet, when it comes to building a legacy that can last for generations, taxes can be one of the heaviest drains on the impact of your hard work.

For 2017, the federal estate exemption was $5.49 million per individual and $10.98 million for a married couple, with estates facing up to a 40 percent tax rate after that. In 2021, those limits increased to $11.7 million for individuals and $23.4 million for married couples, with the 40 percent top level gift and estate tax remaining the same. Currently, the new estate limits are set to increase with inflation until January 1, 2026, when they will "sunset" back to the inflation-adjusted 2017 limits.[46] And that's not taking into account the various state regulations and taxes regarding estate and inheritance transfers.

Another tax concern "frequent flyer": retirement accounts.

---

[46] Laura Sanders, Richard Rubin. The Wall Street Journal. April 8, 2021. "Estate and Gift Taxes 2020-2021: Here's What You Need to Know." https://www.wsj.com/articles/estate-and-gift-taxes-2020-2021-heres-what-you-need-to-know-11617908256

Your IRA or 401(k) can be a source of tax issues when you pass away. For one thing, taking funds from a sizeable account can trigger a large tax bill. However, if you leave the assets in the account, there are still required minimum distributions (RMDs), which will take effect even after you die. If you pass the account to your spouse, he or she can keep taking your RMDs as is, or your spouse can retitle the account in his or her name and receive RMDs based on his or her life expectancy. Remember, if you don't take your RMDs, the IRS will take up to 50 percent of whatever your required distribution was, plus you will still have to pay income taxes whenever you withdraw that money. Thanks to the enactment of the SECURE Act, anyone who inherits your IRA, with few exceptions (your spouse, a beneficiary less than ten years younger, or a disabled adult child, to name a few), will need to empty the account within ten years of your death.[47]

Also—and this is a pretty big also—check with an attorney if you are considering putting your IRA or 401(k) in a trust. An improperly titled beneficiary form for the IRA could mean the difference of thousands of dollars in taxes. This is just one more reason to work with a financial professional, one who can strategically partner with an estate planning attorney to diligently check your decisions.

---

[47] Julia Kagan. Investopedia. October 11, 2020. "Stretch IRA." https://www.investopedia.com/terms/s/stretch-ira.asp

CHAPTER 9
Women Retire Too

We help men, women, and families from all walks of life on their journey to and through retirement. Yet, we want to address the female demographic specifically. Why? To be perfectly blunt, women are more likely to deal with poverty than men when they reach retirement. One report notes that of the people living in poverty in the U.S., 56 percent are women.[48]

The topics, products, and strategies we cover elsewhere in this book are meant to help address retirement concerns for men *and* women, but the dire statistic above is a reminder that much of traditional planning is geared toward men. Male careers, male lifespans, male health care. The bottom line is women's career paths often look much different than men's, so why would their retirement planning look the same?

Women often embrace different roles and values than men as workers, wives, mothers, and daughters. They are more apt to take on roles as caretakers. They often plan for events, worry about loved ones, tend to details, and think about the future. Also, they often want everything to be just right, and they want to be right themselves. It could be you've seen the following affixed to a decorative sign, refrigerator magnet, or T-shirt: "If

---

[48] Robin Bleiweis, Diana Boesch. Center for American Progress. August 3, 2020. "The Basic Facts About Women in Poverty." https://www.americanprogress.org/issues/women/reports/2020/08/03/488536/basic-facts-women-poverty

I agreed with you, we'd both be wrong." The barb features a picture of a woman speaking to a man.

If these characteristics we listed about women are accurate, shouldn't they deserve special considerations from financial professionals? The case can be made, particularly since 70 percent of men in the U.S. age 65 and older happen to be married, compared to 47 percent of women in that age classification.[49] Single women don't have the opportunity to capitalize on the resource pooling and economies of scale accompanying a marriage or partnership.

Be Informed

It's a familiar scene in many financial offices across the country: A woman comes into an appointment carrying a sack full of unopened envelopes. Often through tears, she sits across the desk from a financial professional and apologizes her way through a conversation about what financial products she owns and where her income is coming from. She is recently widowed and was sure her spouse was taking care of the finances, but now she doesn't know where all their assets are kept, and her confidence in her financial outlook has wavered after walking through funeral expenses and realizing she's down to one income.

Often, she may be financially "okay." Yet, the uncertainty can be wearying, particularly when the family is already reeling from a loss. While this scenario sometimes plays out with men, in our experience, it's more likely to be a woman in that chair across from one of our desks, probably, in part, because of Western traditions about money management being "a guy thing." But it doesn't have to be this way. This all-too-common scenario can be wiped away with just a little preparation.

---

[49] Administration for Community Living. May 27, 2021. "Profile of Older Americans." https://acl.gov/aging-and-disability-in-america/data-and-research/profile-older-americans

Talk to Your Spouse/
Work with a Financial Professional

While there are many factors affecting women's financial preparation for and situation in retirement, we cannot emphasize enough that the decision to be informed, to be a part of the conversation, and to be aware of what is going on with your finances is absolutely paramount to a confident retirement. With all the couples we've seen, there is almost always an "alpha" when it comes to finances. It isn't always men—for many of our coupled clients, the wife is the alpha who keeps the books and budgets and knows where all of the family's assets are, down to the penny—yet, statistically, among baby boomers it is usually a man who runs the books. But, as time goes on, it looks like the ratio of male to female financial alphas is evening out. According to a Gallup study, women are equally as likely to take the lead on finances as men, with 37 percent of U.S. households showing women primarily paying the bills. Half of households also say decisions about savings and investments are shared equally.[50] Whether that's the way your household works or not, there isn't anything wrong with who does what.

The breakdown happens when there is a lack of communication, when no one other than the financial alpha knows how much the family has and where. In the end, it doesn't matter who handles the money; it's about all parties being informed of what's going on financially.

There are a lot of ways to open the conversation about money. One woman started a conversation with her husband, the financial alpha, by sitting down and saying, "Teach me how to be a widow." Perhaps that sounds grim, but it was to the point, and it spurred what she said was a very fruitful conversation.

---

[50] Megan Brenan. Gallup. January 29, 2020. "Women Still Handle Main Household Tasks in U.S." https://news.gallup.com/poll/283979/women-handle-main-household-tasks.aspx

They spent a day, just one part of an otherwise dull weekend, going through everything she might need to know. They spent the better part of two decades together after that. When he died, and she was widowed, she said the "widowhood" talk had made a huge difference. She knew who to call to talk through their retirement plan and where to call for the insurance policy.

Years later, she accompanied a recently widowed friend of hers to a financial appointment. Her friend was emotional the whole time, afraid she would run out of money any day. The financial professional ultimately showed the friend that she was financially in good shape, but not before the friend had already spent months worried that each check would exhaust her bank account. That's no way to live after losing a loved one. It was preventable had her deceased spouse and financial professional included her in a conversation about "widowhood."

Couples sometimes have their first real conversation about money, assets, and their retirement income approach, in our office. The important thing about having these conversations isn't where, it's when ... and the best "when" is as soon as possible.

Spouse-Specific Options

One area where it might be especially important to be on the same page between spouses is when it comes to financial products or services that have spousal options. A few that come to mind are pensions and Social Security, although life insurance and annuity policies also have the potential to affect both spouses.

With pensions, taking the worker's life-only option is somewhat attractive—after all, the monthly payment is bigger. However, you and your spouse should discuss your options. When we're talking about both of you, as opposed to just one lifespan, there is an increased likelihood at least one of you will live a long, long time. This means the monthly payout will be less, but it also ensures that, no matter which spouse outlives the other, no one will have to suffer the loss of a needed pension paycheck in his or her later retirement years.

While we covered Social Security options in a different chapter, we think some of the spousal information bears repeating. Particularly, if you worked exclusively inside the home for a significant number of years, you may want to talk about taking your Social Security benefits based on your spouse's work history. After all, Social Security is based on your thirty-five highest-earning years.

Things to remember about the spousal benefits:[51]
- Your benefit will be calculated as a percentage (up to 50 percent) of your spouse's earned monthly benefit at his or her full retirement age, or FRA.
- For you to begin receiving a spousal benefit, your spouse must have already filed for his or her own benefits and you must be at least sixty-two.
- You can qualify for a full half of your spouse's benefits if you wait until you reach FRA to file.
- Beginning your benefits earlier than your FRA will reduce your monthly check but waiting to file until after FRA will not increase your benefits.

For divorcees:[52]
- You may qualify for an ex-spousal benefit if . . .
    a. You were married for a decade or more
    b. *and* you are at least sixty-two
    c. *and* you have been divorced for at least two years
    d. *and* you are currently unmarried
    e. *and* your ex-spouse is sixty-two (qualifies to begin taking Social Security)

---

[51] Social Security Administration. "Retirement Planner: Benefits For You As A Spouse." https://www.ssa.gov/planners/retire/applying6.html
[52] Social Security Administration. "Retirement Planner: If You Are Divorced." https://www.ssa.gov/planners/retire/divspouse.html

- Your ex-spouse does not need to have filed for you to file on his or her benefit.
- Similar to spousal benefits, you can qualify for up to half of your ex-spouse's benefits if you wait to file until your FRA.
- If your ex-spouse dies, you may file to receive a widow/widower benefit on his or her Social Security record as long as you are at least age sixty and fulfill all the other requirements on the preceding alphabetized list.
    a. This will not affect the benefits of your ex-spouse's current spouse

For widow's (or widower's, for that matter) benefits:[53]
- You may qualify to receive as much as your deceased spouse would have received if . . .
    a. You were married for at least nine months before his or her death
    b. *or* you would qualify for a divorced spousal benefit
    c. *and* you are at least sixty
    d. *and* you did not/have not remarried before age sixty
- You may earn delayed credits on your spouse's benefit *if* your spouse hadn't already filed for benefits when he or she died.
- Other rules may apply to you if you are disabled or are caring for a deceased spouse's dependent or disabled child.

---

[53] Social Security Administration. "Survivors Planner: If You Are The Worker's Widow Or Widower." https://www.ssa.gov/planners/survivors/ifyou.html#h2

Longevity

On average, women live longer than men. Most stats put average female longevity at about two years more than men. But averages are tricky things. A more telling statistic that surfaced in 2010 U.S. Census data revealed that more than 80 percent of U.S. centenarians, those over 100, are women. That means the vast majority of the eldest elderly are women.[54] The Population Reference Bureau projects women 85 and older will compose almost 2.9 percent of the U.S. population in 2060 and outnumber girls age zero to four (2.7 percent).

On one hand, this is a Brandi Chastain moment. You know, when the American soccer icon shed her jersey to celebrate a game-winning penalty kick to win the World Cup. Seriously, how fabulous are women? They tend to be meticulous, resolute, perseverant. On the other hand, the trend for women to live longer presents longstanding financial ramifications.

Simply Needing More Money in Retirement

Living longer in retirement means needing more money, period. Barring a huge lottery win or some crazy stock market action, the date you retire is likely the point at which you have the most money you will ever have. Not to put too grim a spin on it, but the problem with longevity is, the further you get away from that date, the further your dollars have to stretch. If you planned to live to a nice eighty-something but live to a nice one-hundred-something, that is *two decades* you will need to account for, monetarily.

To put this in perspective, let's say you like to drink coffee as an everyday splurge. Not accounting for inflation or leap years, a $2.50 cup-a-day habit is $18,250 over a two-decade span.

---

[54] U.S. Census Bureau. December 10, 2012. "2010 Census Report Shows More Than 80 Percent of Centenarians are Women." https://www.census.gov/newsroom/releases/archives/2010_census/cb12-239.html

Now, think of all the things you like to do that cost money. Add those up for twenty years of unanticipated costs. We think you'll see what we mean.

During the 2020 onset of the coronavirus pandemic, many learned to cut costs. For some, that amounted to skipping their decadent latte. For others, however, cutbacks became acute. According to data compiled by Age Wave and Edward Jones, 32 percent of Americans plan to retire later than planned because of the pandemic. Women felt a more adverse effect. The report stipulated that 41 percent of women continued to save for retirement, compared to 58 percent of men.[55]

Yet women often tend to be planners, and during prosperous times that do not include, oh, a pandemic, they participate in retirement plans at rates 5 to 14 percentage points higher than men. Less earnings, however, often reduce the amounts women can contribute to such plans.[56]

More Health Care Needs

In addition to the cost of living for a longer lifespan is the fact aging, plain and simple, means more health care, and more health care means more money. Women are survivors. They suffer from the morbidity-mortality paradox, which states women suffer more non-fatal illnesses throughout their lifetime than men, who experience fewer illnesses but higher mortality.

Women have been found to seek treatment more often when not feeling well and emphasize staying healthy when older,

---

[55] Megan Leonhardt. cnbc.com. June 16, 2021. "58% of men were able to continue saving for retirement during the pandemic—but only 41% of women were." https://www.cnbc.com/2021/06/16/why-pandemic-hit-womens-retirement-savings-more-than-mens.html

[56] Hana Polyak. cnbc.com. March 2, 2020. "With less savings and longer lifespan, women must take 4 key steps to shore up retirement." https://www.cnbc.com/2020/02/28/longer-lifespan-fueling-women-to-take-key-steps-to-shore-up-retirement.html

according to studies.[57] So survival is on the side of the woman. However, surviving things, like cancer, also means more checkups later in life.

Widowhood

Not only do women typically live longer than their same-age male counterparts, they also have the tendency to marry men older than themselves. The numbers bear this out: Women are four times more likely to outlive their spouses than men.[58]

We don't write this to scare people; rather, we think it's fundamentally important to prepare our female clients for something that may be a startling, *but very likely,* scenario. At some point, most women will have to handle their financial situations on their own. A little preparation can go a long way, and having a basic understanding of your household finances and the "who, what, where, and how much" of your family's assets is incredibly useful—it can prevent a tragic situation from being more traumatic.

In our opinion, the financial services industry sometimes underserves women in these situations. Some financial professionals tend to alienate women, even when their spouses are alive. We've heard several stories of women who sat through meeting after meeting without their financial professional ever addressing a single question to them.

In our firm, when we work with couples, we work hard to make sure our retirement income strategies work for *both* people. No matter who is the financial alpha, it's important for everyone who is affected by a retirement strategy to understand it.

---

[57] advisory.com. July 22, 2020. "Why do women live longer than men? It's more complicated than you think." https://www.advisory.com/en/daily-briefing/2020/07/22/longevity

[58] Jean Chatzky. thebalance.com. January 30, 2021. "How Women Can Plan for Outliving Their Husbands." https://www.thebalance.com/retirement-plan-for-women-outliving-husbands-4139845

We've seen the importance of this need firsthand with our Grandma Irma. Our grandpa (Dave Sr.'s father) passed away following a heart attack in his early sixties, leaving Grandma on her own for thirty-plus years.

We believe the biggest need for widows is having a plan in place that they and their spouse understand to help ensure their assets will last for the rest of their lives.

In many marriages, men implement the financial plan, but they never know if it actually worked. Because women generally live longer, they're usually the ones who are around to see if there's enough money for their eighties and nineties.

Our grandma was very fortunate because Dad's job was in retirement planning. So, she had the resources and knowledge from her son. She wasn't scrambling around to go figure everything out. Unfortunately, that's not the case for most people. As mentioned earlier in this chapter, it's all too common for widows to be completely overwhelmed with their finances once their husband is gone.

To help combat this lack of communication and ensure a husband and wife are both in the know on financial matters, we give every family a binder with all of their important documents inside. This includes account numbers, a guide to locating important accounts and assets, and a detailed plan on what to do after one spouse passes.

We also provide a survivor's checklist, which helps give widows a general guide of what to do first in a time that can be very challenging and confusing. This checklist breaks down what to do within thirty days, within sixty days, and within six months. We've included this checklist on the following pages.

CAPITAL A
Wealth Management

A Survivor's Checklist
Things that need to be done when a loved one dies
Keep with your important papers

IMMEDIATE:

	Obtain signed death certificate and autopsy (If applicable).
	Within the first 24 hours, look for organ donation records. Check for signed authorizations and arrange immediately.
	Inventory safe deposit boxes and personal papers of the deceased. Look for burial insurance policies, prepaid mortuary or cremation society plans.
	Contact mortuary to make burial (or cremation) and funeral arrangements. Arrange for obituary notice.
	Contact friends and relatives. ALLOW YOUR FRIENDS AND RELATIVES TO HELP YOU OUT IN THIS TIME OF NEED.
	Make arrangements for pets (if any).
	Cancel regular elder assistance services, if any (such as Meals on Wheels).
	Obtain certified copies of the death certificate from the mortuary (consider purchasing 10 to 20 copies).

WITHIN 30 DAYS:

If Applicable, Notify:

	Social Security Administration to stop checks
	Appropriate agency if receiving health care benefits through a governmental program
	Veterans Administration
	Payers of Pensions (such as former employer) or annuities
	Department of Motor Vehicles

What Documentation to Locate:

	Will
	Trust(s)
	Insurance policies
	Deeds to real estate

If Living Trust, Notify:

	Successor Trustee (Trust Manager) for eventual distribution of assets
	Attorney
	Insurance companies and arrange for any death benefits to be paid to beneficiaries
	IRA and pension companies for any death benefits to be paid to beneficiaries

If NO Living Trust and ONLY a will, Notify:

	County clerk and deposit the original will within 30 days
	Executor to begin and probate process with an attorney
	Capital A Wealth Management at 724.658.4211 for review of possible death and/or income owing and assistance in sorting out and distributing assets

WITHIN 60 DAYS:
Notify all creditors and utility companies.
Transfer title on jointly held assets.
Inventory personal effects and arrange for disposition to family members, friends or charities.

WITHIN 6 MONTHS:
If Surviving Spouse:
Contact Capital A Wealth Management at 724.658.4211 for review of finances and revised financial game plan.
Update your will or trust.

This material is for informational purposes only. It is not intended to provide legal advice or provide the basis for any financial decisions. You are encouraged to consult with an attorney before making decisions about your individual situation.

Taxes

One of the often-unexpected aspects of widowhood is the tax bill. Many women continue similar lifestyles to the ones they shared with their spouses. This, in turn, means continuing to have a similar need for income. However, after the death of a spouse, their taxes will be calculated based on a single filer's income table, which is much less forgiving than the couple's tax rates. With proper planning, your financial professional and tax advisor may be able to help you take the sting out of your new tax status.

Caregiving

Of the 53 million caregivers providing unpaid, informal care for older adults, 61 percent are women. Among today's family caregivers, 61 percent work and 45 percent report some kind of financial impact from providing a loved one care and support.[59] In addition to the financial burden created by caregiving responsibilities, women devote an average of forty hours each week to unpaid work when adding duties such as

---

[59] caregiving.org. 2020 Report. "Caregiving in the U.S. 2020." https://www.caregiving.org/caregiving-in-the-us-2020

housekeeping.[60] So then, when can women find the time to focus long and hard on financial matters?

Unfortunately, the impact and hardships created by traditional roles for women typically do not account for Social Security benefit losses or the losses of health care benefits and retirement savings. This also doesn't account for maternity care, mothers who homeschool, or women who leave the workforce to care for their children in any way.

We don't repeat these statistics to scare you. Estimates typically place the monetary value of unofficial caregiving services across the United States at around $150 billion or more. Yet, we think the emotional value of the care many women provide their elderly relatives or neighbors cannot be quantified. So, to be clear, this shouldn't be taken as a "why not to provide caregiving" spiel. Instead, it should be seen as a call for "why to *prepare* for caregiving" or "how to lessen the financial and emotional burden of caregiving."

Funding Your Own Retirement

For these reasons, women need to be prepared to fund more of their own retirements. There are several savings options and products, including the spousal 401(k). Unlike a traditional 401(k), where you contribute money to a plan with your employer, a spousal 401(k) is something your spouse sets up on your behalf, so he or she can contribute a portion of the paycheck to your retirement funds. This is something to consider, particularly for families where one spouse has dropped out of the workforce to care for a relative.

Also, if you find yourself in a caregiving role, talk to your employer's human resources department. Some companies have paid leave, special circumstance, or sick leave options you

---

[60] Drew Weisholtz. Today. January 22, 2020. "Women do 2 more hours of housework daily than men, study says."
https://www.today.com/news/women-do-2-more-hours-housework-daily-men-study-says-t172272

could qualify for, making it easier to cope and helping you stay in the workforce longer.

Saving Money

Women need more money to fund their retirements, period. But this doesn't have to be a significant burden—most of the time, women are better at saving, while usually taking less risk in their portfolios.[61] This gives us reason to believe, as women get more involved in their finances, families will continue to be better-prepared for retirement, both *his* and *hers*.

---

[61] Maurie Backman. The Motley Fool. March 4, 2021. "A Summary of 20 Years of Research and Statistics on Women in Investing." https://www.fool.com/research/women-in-investing-research

CHAPTER 10

Long-Term Care Insurance

Elsewhere in this book, we've outlined the risks longevity poses to your financial health. In fact, you may be tired of hearing it at this point.

Even so, we'd still like to repeat one more time—in case you've forgotten—it's estimated *seven* out of every ten Americans who reach age sixty-five will need long-term care of some kind.[62] Let us ask, if you knew the car you were going to be riding in had a 70 percent chance of having an accident, would you wear your seatbelt?

The bottom line is we need to do a better job of planning for the possibility of long-term care. A public poll of Americans recently revealed nearly two-thirds of the public (63 percent) favor more involvement from the federal government to help provide health insurance for more Americans.[63] However, if you think about the current problems plaguing government-run programs such as Social Security, Medicaid, and Medicare, we think it stands to reason, for the time being, we're probably on our own.

---

[62] LongTermCare.gov. February 18, 2020. "How Much Care Will You Need?" https://acl.gov/ltc/basic-needs/how-much-care-will-you-need

[63] Bradley Jones. Pew Research Center. September 29, 2020. "Increasing share of Americans favor a single government program to provide health care coverage" https://www.pewresearch.org/fact-tank/2020/09/29/increasing-share-of-americans-favor-a-single-government-program-to-provide-health-care-coverage

Elsewhere, we covered the various ways of preparing for our own possible long-term care costs, from self-funding to insurance riders. We'd like to take a moment to expand on what is one of the most comprehensive coverage options: long-term care insurance.

LTCI Basics

The long-term care insurance, or LTCI, space has had a bit of a shakeup in the past few years. Many insurers stopped offering LTCI, and the policies remaining are often more expensive. In addition, denials of LTCI applications have risen to the point almost one-third of those between ages sixty and sixty-five are rejected.[64]

Yet, the other side of the coin is the insurers who are left in the LTCI space have experience and policies that have endured. LTCI may be more expensive for individuals, but that's because they can be more expensive for insurers and because overall long-term care is just plain expensive, period. It's important to understand LTCI carriers aren't just making money hand-over-fist with these products. Instead, the carriers who have stopped selling policies were likely carriers who had unrealistic prices and underperforming policies. Unfortunately, it looks like the current market might only get more expensive in the next few decades.[65]

While many criticize the use-it-or-lose-it nature of LTCI, it is reasonable to consider that homeowner's insurance, car insurance, term life insurance, and many other types of insurance work the same way. Yes, you are paying into a policy in the hopes you may never use it. But, if you must use it, it can

---

[64] Alexander Sammon. The American Prospect. October 20, 2020. "The Collapse of Long-Term Care Insurance."
https://prospect.org/familycare/the-collapse-of-long-term-care-insurance
[65] American Association for Long-Term Care Insurance. January 12, 2021. "2021 Long Term Care Insurance Price Index Released."
https://www.aaltci.org/news/long-term-care-insurance-association-news/2021-long-term-care-insurance-price-index-released-for-age-55

provide value well beyond the actual dollars you have paid into it. With an average of 353,100 home fires every year for the 128.45 million households in the United States, you have *less than a half a percent chance* of experiencing a home fire in any given year.[66, 67] Most of us would still squirm at the thought of not having homeowner's or renter's insurance to cover fire damage, however. Paradoxically, even with the statistics from the U.S. Department of Health and Human Services estimating we each have a *70 percent chance* of needing long-term care, only 7 percent of Americans have LTCI.[68, 69]

To purchase LTCI, you have to complete an application that includes a medical questionnaire. Depending on your age and the insurance carrier, you may also need to complete a medical exam. If you qualify, then the insurance company will offer you a policy with certain coverage and pricing based in part on your odds of needing long-term care in the future. The younger you are, the more likely you are to qualify—at a rate that is more likely affordable for you.

LTCI premiums count as medical expenses and may potentially be paid with special tax considerations. For instance, if you are eligible to itemize your medical expenses, LTCI premiums can be itemized. Or, alternately, you can pay premiums with tax-free money in health savings accounts. The amount you can withdraw tax-free for LTCI premiums depends on your age.

---

[66] Marty Ahrens. National Fire Prevention Association. November 2020. "Home Structure Fires." https://www.nfpa.org/News-and-Research/Data-research-and-tools/Building-and-Life-Safety/Home-Structure-Fires

[67] Statista. 2021. "Number of households in the U.S. from 1960 to 2020 (in millions)." https://www.statista.com/statistics/183635/number-of-households-in-the-us

[68] Diane Omdahl. Forbes. January 14, 2020. "Does Medicare Pay For Long-Term Care? Don't Make A Big Mistake." https://www.forbes.com/sites/dianeomdahl/2020/01/14/does-medicare-pay-for-long-term-care-dont-make-a-big-mistake/#f30eee411f39

[69] Alexander Sammon. The American Prospect. October 20, 2020. "The Collapse of Long-Term Care Insurance." https://prospect.org/familycare/the-collapse-of-long-term-care-insurance

If you have an LTCI policy, coverage will typically kick in when you have been medically shown to be unable to perform two or more activities of daily living (ADLs). An ADL is an activity such as bathing, toileting, eating, dressing, grooming, etc. These are all things we naturally prefer to do by ourselves; they are markers of our independence and ability to take care of ourselves. Once someone is unable to do some of these things alone, they need long-term help. So, if you have LTCI, once you reach this point you will qualify for a daily amount of coverage over a pre-selected time period, depending on the terms of your policy. That money could be used to cover a nursing home, in-home care, or community organization care. The benefits will begin after the policy's elimination period, which you choose when you purchase the policy. The elimination period can range from 0 to 180 days, and the shorter the elimination period, the higher the premium.

With LTCI, you can pick and choose facilities or care options according to your standards instead of having the government decide what is best for you.

Long-Term Care Partnership Program

One other significant advantage of LTCI is many plans are eligible for a federal-state government initiative called the Long-Term Care Partnership Program.[70] This program is a joint effort by the federal government and certain states to help individuals decide to choose LTCI protection. It means, if you deplete your LTCI coverage and find yourself in a position of having to spend down your assets to become eligible for Medicaid, part or all of your LTCI coverage limit will extend to your assets. Here's what this might look like "in real life" (using, of course, a completely hypothetical person):

---

[70] American Association for Long-Term Care Insurance. 2022. "Long Term Care Insurance Partnership Plans." http://www.aaltci.org/long-term-care-insurance/learning-center/long-term-care-insurance-partnership-plans.php

Jennifer chooses an LTCI policy to cover up to three years of nursing home care (a little more than the average long-term care stay) in a semi-private room. After several injuries render her unable to dress or bathe herself, Jennifer moves to Winters Retirement Community. Jennifer is not average. Her policy has paid out more than $250,000 on her behalf, and her policy benefits are now exhausted. This puts her in position for a Medicaid spend down. However, because she purchased a policy her state approved in line with the Long-Term Care Partnership Program, instead of having to spend down her assets to the Medicaid requirement and leaving very little for her family to inherit, she is allowed to set aside $250,000 on top of her state's other spend-down exemptions.

When we recommend long-term care insurance for our clients, we often use what's called a LTC/life insurance combination policy. With traditional long-term care, if you pass away before using your coverage, the money you paid into the policy may be lost. In a combo policy, any remaining death benefit can be passed down tax-free to properly named beneficiaries.

We feel this is the best way to plan for long-term care in most instances. You do have to go through underwriting for this type of policy, so there are other ways to pay for it. But because health care costs can be very expensive, we like the combination policies.

LTCI — It's Not Just About You

Aside from the aforementioned partnership program and possible tax advantages of traditional LTCI, I think perhaps one of the most compelling arguments in favor of preparing for the likelihood of long-term care has less to do with our own personal assets and more to do with others.

What do we mean? Well, we hear from lots of people who think it won't matter. "Oh, by the time I reach the point of needing long-term care, I'll be out of my mind. Who cares who takes care of me and how that happens?"

However, like estate planning, long-term care planning isn't solely about us. In fact, we might argue that the most important piece of long-term care planning isn't about you at all. It's about your loved ones. It's about your spouse, your children, or your friends, and how caring for you could impact them if you don't have the necessary resources.

Most caregiving for the elderly happens in people's private homes. A 2021 survey of caregivers reveals just a sampling of how a long stint of caring for relatives and loved ones can affect the caregivers:[71]

- Of those surveyed, a mean of nineteen hours a week was provided in care. Among those, about 38 percent had to cut back their hours at their job
- 66 percent of caregivers used their personal assets, like savings and retirement funds, to pay for a loved one's care
- 52 percent of caregivers moved closer to the loved one for whom they provided care

Because of its benefits for both the policy holder and his or her family or caregiver, LTCI can be a valuable asset in any retirement plan.

---

[71] Genworth. November 16, 2021. "Beyond Dollars 2021." https://pro.genworth.com/riiproweb/productinfo/pdf/682801BRO.pdf

CHAPTER 11

Finding a Financial Professional

In the opening chapter, we mentioned that when we joined our dad's business, we decided to rename the firm "Capital A Wealth Management" to honor his middle initial and the nickname he often answers to: "A."

When we were growing up, everyone would come up to us and say how much our dad helped them make sound financial decisions. That inspired us to take a similar approach in our careers because we saw and heard firsthand how working in this industry can help change people's lives.

Through his decades of experience, Dad got his processes down to a science. One of our goals when we joined the firm was to extract those methods and turn them into a quantifiable, deliverable system that can be of use to any client who walks through our door.

As a result, the principles and values Dad brought to David A. Domenick Investments will remain in place for many more years to come.

We both joined the team shortly after graduating college, Dave in 2013 and Brandon in 2017, after brief stops at larger, big-name financial companies. After seeing how our dad ran things, we didn't like the mindset in these cold, corporate settings. While working for a nationally known life insurance firm, a common question from management was, "How many lives did you get today?" We believe treating people as a number is no way to do business. As independent financial professionals, we put clients' needs first.

We aim to provide what we call the three C's: Confidence, Comfort, and Control. Everyone has unique goals and financial situations, but one thing all people have in common is they want to know that they're on the right track for retirement. Some may simply want financial stability, others may prefer the high-risk, high-reward potential of the stock market. Either way, with a proper, well-laid-out plan, anyone can have financial confidence, knowing a downturn in the stock market doesn't have to prompt a negative, emotional reaction. It's all about what your level of comfort is.

Nobody is more familiar with your comfort level and areas of concern as you are. However, that can make it difficult to separate emotion from your financial decisions. That's one reason we believe it's important to work with a financial professional.

Finances and retirement planning are ever-changing, and it's a lot for any one person to keep up on. Just think about some of the factors at play in 2022: We're currently in a low interest rate environment, coming off a period when the market's been up for twelve years and counting. People are living a lot longer and tax rate changes are likely on the horizon.

Because of these headwinds, we believe professional guidance is more important than ever. We meet a lot of people who get their financial wisdom from a relative or neighbor. The downside of that is, not everyone's the same. What worked for your neighbor may not work for you, in part because you likely have very different goals.

If you and your neighbor both had check-ups with the doctor, you wouldn't receive the same prescriptions, right? Maybe you're healthy and your neighbor has nagging health issues, or vice versa. We're not all the same, and therefore, you're not going to walk away with the same medications.

Along those same lines, a cookie-cutter approach doesn't work for financial health, either. The people who see us won't leave with the commonplace 60/40 split of stocks and bonds unless that combination truly helps them meet their unique goals.

Another thing to keep in mind is that a second opinion never hurts. Even if you've already been working with another financial firm, the strategy that got you to retirement may not be the best one once you've stopped working. We like to view advisors in two distinct categories: those who focus on accumulation and those who focus on the distribution.

Both are important at different phases of life. Accumulation is all about growing your assets, and distribution is all about spending those assets in a way that helps ensure they last a lifetime. Our focus is on distribution in your retirement years, which means taking a comprehensive look beyond just which investments will make you the most money.

Think about it like this: When you go to the doctor, you don't see a pediatrician anymore. Once you reach a certain age, you move onto a specialist who can better meet your current needs. Like a doctor who focuses on a specialized field, we work specifically with clients who are closing in on retirement.

Our mission statement is to inspire our clients one appointment, one review, and one conversation at a time. We want to help people in our communities live the most empowered retirement possible.

We wrote this book to provide an introductory overview of our financial philosophies, but only by meeting in person can we create a strategy tailored to your specific financial needs. Thanks for reading, and we hope for the opportunity to help make your retirement dreams a reality.

Acknowledgments

First and foremost, we must thank our dad for having the vision and determination to lay the groundwork for what Capital A Wealth Management is today.

We're grateful for the opportunity to manage the firm as equal partners with Michael Richards and Joe Palimino. Together, we hope to meet the high standards set by our father years ago and provide the level of service the people we work with have come to expect.

This business would not exist without our clients, and every day, we're thankful we have the ability to help people like you take the next step toward the retirement of your dreams.

CAPITAL A WEALTH MANAGEMENT
About the Authors

David Domenick Jr.
Managing Partner

David is a graduate of Indiana University of Pennsylvania, where he received his Bachelor of Science degree in finance and legal studies. While attending IUP, he earned his Bloomberg Certifications, also known as Bloomberg Market Concepts (BMC), an e-learning course that provides an introduction to the context of financial markets and practices using Bloomberg terminal. Upon graduation, began his career in the financial services industry.

David maintains his FINRA Series 7 and 66 securities registrations and is a Registered Representative of Madison Avenue Securities, LLC and an Investment Adviser Representative of AE Wealth Management. He is also licensed in life, accident, and health insurance.

David enjoys spending time with friends and family and being active in the community.

Brandon Domenick
Managing Partner

Brandon began his career in the financial industry after earning a Bachelor of Science in business administration from Westminster College. He maintains his FINRA Series 65 investment advisor registration through AE Wealth Management and is also licensed in life, accident, and health insurance.

Outside the office, Brandon enjoys spending time with friends and family, playing basketball and being active in the community.

Made in the USA
Middletown, DE
22 September 2022